ONE DOOR CLOSES ANOTHER OPENS

Bernadette O'Sullivan rsj

© Trustees of the Sisters of Saint Joseph 2018. All rights reserved.

Except as provided by the Copyright Act 1968, no part of this publication may be reproduced, stored in a retrieval system or transmitted in any forms or by any means without prior written permission of the publisher.

Series Editors: Josephite Editorial Committee
The Josephite Series offers contributions on various aspects of:
Theology and spirituality
Historical perspectives
Cultures and life experiences, and Faith communities.

1. *In the Land of Larks and Heroes: Australian Reflections on St Mary MacKillop*, edited by Alan Cadwallader, 2011.
2. *St Joseph's Island: Julian Tenison Woods and the Tasmanian Sisters of St Joseph*, Josephine Margaret Brady rsj, 2012.
3. *God's Good Time: The Journey of the Sisters of St Joseph of the Sacred Heart in Ministry with Australian Aboriginal and Torres Strait Islander Peoples*, Mary Cresp rsj, 2013.
4. *Never See a Need: The Sisters of St Joseph in South Australia 1866–2010*, Marie Therese Foale rsj, 2016.
5. *Mary MacKillop 1873: One Year of an Extraordinary Life*, Sheila McCreanor rsj, 2016.
6. *A Priceless Treasure: Sister Teresa McDonald Pioneer Sister of St Joseph 1838–1876*, Marie Crowley, 2016.
7. *Fire in the Red Land: A Two-Act Play on the Life of Saint Mary of the Cross MacKillop*, Margaret Therese Cusack rsj, 2017.
8. *A Faith-Filled Family: Mary MacKillop's Sisters and Brothers*, Judith Geddes rsj, 2017.

ISBN: 978-1-925643-66-4 (paperback)
        978-1-925643-67-1(hardback)
        978-1-925643-69-5 (ebook : epub)

Text Minion Pro Size 10 & 11.

Published by:

An imprint of the ATF Press Publishing
Group owned by ATF (Australia) Ltd.
PO Box 504
Hindmarsh, SA 5007
ABN 90 116 359 963
www.atfpress.com
Making a lasting impact

ONE DOOR CLOSES ANOTHER OPENS

Mary MacKillop in New South Wales 1880–1909

Bernadette O'Sullivan rsj

Adelaide
2018

Table of Contents

Foreword		vii
Introduction		ix
Chapter One:	A Door Closes in Queensland, Opens in New South Wales	1
Chapter Two:	1880, A Year of Foundations	5
Chapter Three:	Developments, 1881–1883	19
Chapter Four:	1885, A Memorable Year	43
Chapter Five:	Joys and Sorrows of 1886	57
Chapter Six:	New Beginnings in 1887	67
Chapter Seven:	Many Foundations in 1888 and Good News from Rome	75
Chapter Eight:	The Years 1890–1892	87
Chapter Nine:	Events of 1893–1895	99
Chapter Ten:	A Round of Visits	107
Chapter Eleven:	Death and a New Beginning, 1898–1899	119
Chapter Twelve:	More Foundations in 1900 and 1901	129
Chapter Thirteen:	Mary MacKillop's Three Week Visitation of the South–East of NSW	141
Chapter Fourteen:	Other Foundations in 1901 and 1902	147
Chapter Fifteen:	The Final Years, 1903–1909	159
Reflection:	A Time to Reap	177

Appendices:

Appendix One:	Sisters Named in text	181
Appendix Two:	Map of New South Wales showing Foundations 1880–1909	187
Appendix Three:	Buildings at Mount Street North Sydney: 1884–1909	189
Appendix Four:	Means of Transport	193
Bibliography		195

Foreword

The title of this book 'One Door Closes Another Opens' immediately engages the reader in a story that tells of a journey of letting go of a current reality and welcoming the new. It connects the reader with the reality that in the midst of suffering, hope is born and new life emerges.

The story begins with the departure of the Sisters of St Joseph from Queensland in 1880. It was with heavy hearts that Sisters who had lived and worked there for ten years, and had had many struggles with Bishop James Quinn, finally chose to leave all behind because of their commitment to the centrally-governed Religious Congregation founded by Mary MacKillop and Fr Julian Tenison Woods. Mary MacKillop herself was deeply affected by this experience. As Sister Bernadette O'Sullivan tells us, when the Sisters were leaving, Mary MacKillop broke down in tears.

When the Sisters arrived in Sydney, they were welcomed with open arms by Archbishop Vaughan who was seeking Religious to teach in the Catholic schools in his diocese. Bishop Torreggiani of Armidale was also delighted to welcome some of the Sisters into his diocese. These Sisters were well trained teachers who had done a great deal to establish Catholic schools in Queensland. What a gift and a blessing! And so began a story of flourishment—out of the hardship and tears of one experience came the joy and the challenge of making new foundations across New South Wales.

In this book Sr Bernadette invites us to journey with Mary MacKillop into the many scattered communities of New South Wales—into city schools, rural communities and outback towns from 1880–1909. Her journey began in a stable school in Penrith, replicating the story of the first St Joseph's School at Penola in South Australia. Like all the pioneering Sisters, the women who formed the first community at Penrith were prepared to live in poor circumstances in order to provide a Catholic education for the children of this region. The book is full of stories of such openings and tells of how Mary MacKillop journeyed, often under difficult circumstances, to support and encourage the Sisters in their commitment and mission, to spend time with the people among whom they lived and to share in their daily lives. Sometimes it meant her staying overnight in a hotel on her way to a distant destination.

The reader will gain many insights by reading the numerous quotations taken from letters and records kept by the Sisters. So many spoke of Mary's kindness, of her attentiveness to their needs, of her words of encouragement and comfort and her sense of humour. Her kindness is reflected through simple actions such as replacing the worn clothing of the Sisters in Tingha, buying a box of Dominoes for the Sisters in Bombala or purchasing a type-writer to make another Sister's work easier. As Sister Bernadette has written: '*Nothing escaped her attention, neither school reports, nor anything to do with the sisters and their schools. She knew that the unity of the sisters would be ensured by her constancy in visitation, and when she could not visit, by her circular letters and her very personal letters that flowed from her busy pen to individual sisters. Few, if any, letters from the sisters remained unanswered. If she was unable to write a letter to a sister she sent a message to her by another sister*'.

In many different places, especially in the country, the Sisters raised money for their support by preparing the children for concerts. While these concerts were usually fund-raisers they often added a cultural richness to the small communities where they were held.

Overall this book tells the story of Mary MacKillop's accompaniment of the members of those early communities of Sisters in New South Wales. It is enriched by personal insights shared in letters. Through it you will encounter Mary's warmth, fortitude, compassion, kindness and resilience. It is a story of joys and sorrows lovingly embraced as, through Mary MacKillop's encouragement, the Sisters brought faith, education and extended works of charity and social service to the people of New South Wales.

May you draw from her story and the story of the Sisters from 1880–1909, the wisdom and courage to meet the challenges of daily life. May you, like them, be inspired to go out and make a difference in the world.

Sr Monica Cavanagh
Congregational Leader

Introduction

The idea of exploring the life of Mary MacKillop in New South Wales came from the members of the Mary MacKillop Committee. Several sisters were active in researching and recording the years 1880–1909 and I was asked to bring this to fruition. Research for these years had been undertaken by Lynette Raftery rsj, Barbara White rsj and Clare Burgess rsj and I have added my own research. Bridie O'Connell's reflection on the final years of Mary MacKillop's life provides a fitting conclusion to the story.

This book, *One Door Closes Another Opens*, aims to tell of the endeavours of Mary MacKillop in spreading the Gospel, sending out her sisters to care for and educate the neglected children in the poorest areas of the city of Sydney, particularly the slum areas around the part known as The Rocks on the shores of Sydney Harbour. These pioneer sisters were sent, too, to far flung towns and villages throughout New South Wales in the Dioceses of Sydney and Armidale, both of which encompassed huge areas. Mary visited the sisters, supported, encouraged, and assisted them in their work for God and his people. She journeyed by every known conveyance then available, in every kind of weather, often enduring snow, torrents of rain, blazing sun and heat and very often suffering poor health. All this was for the glory of her good God and for his children and to bring the message of his love and mercy to people in these isolated places.

The withdrawal of Mary MacKillop's sisters from Bathurst in 1876 closed their work there but it also saw the birth of a diocesan congregation of the Sisters of St Joseph under Bishop Quinn. The Bathurst story has been well told by Dr Marie Crowley in her notable work *Women of the Vale* which is highly recommended to readers.[1]

When Mary MacKillop and her sisters withdrew from Queensland at the end of 1879, they were welcomed into New South Wales by Archbishop Vaughan of Sydney and Bishop Torreggiani of Armidale. Hence the title, *One Door Closes Another Opens*.

This work is a story of heroism, not only on the part of Mary, but also on the part of those pioneer sisters and the generous people who supported them. All of them laboured to teach and strengthen the catholic faith wherever they lived and worked. We thank God for them and dedicate this work to their memory.

I wish to acknowledge the assistance given by Mr Gary Hayes who read the original draft of this work and gave many helpful suggestions. Sister Marie Therese Foale rsj gave of her time and considerable talents as an author to help to bring the work to a conclusion. To them, my grateful thanks.

Bernadette O'Sullivan rsj

---

1. Marie Crowley, *Women of the Vale: Perthville Josephites 1872–1972*, (Melbourne, Spectrum Publications 2002)

MARY MACKILLOP IN NEW SOUTH WALES 1880–1909
Bernadette O'Sullivan rsj

Mary MacKillop.

Chapter One
A Door Closes in Queensland, Opens in New South Wales

At the request of Bishop James Quinn, the sisters, with Mary MacKillop as their leader, journeyed from Adelaide to Brisbane in late December 1869. They established themselves in Brisbane and Mary remained there until April 1871 when she returned to Adelaide, leaving Sister Clare Wright as Provincial. Bishop Quinn was in Europe during Mary's time in Brisbane. When he returned he made it quite clear to Sister Clare and the sisters that he did not accept Central Government and thereafter tried to persuade them to accept him as their sole Superior. This brought about a confrontation with Mary who met him in Brisbane in May 1875.

Between Mary's departure from Brisbane in 1871 and her visit there in 1875, she had been excommunicated and later reinstated, had travelled to Rome and returned with Constitutions that were in a format suitable for a religious congregation with Central Government and that had been affirmed there. However, the strict poverty outlined in the Rule that she took to Rome had been modified to allow the sisters to possess property. As instructed by the officials in Rome, the first General Chapter was held in Kensington, South Australia from 19–23 March 1875. At this Chapter the Constitutions Mary brought from Rome were accepted unanimously and subsequently the sisters then in South Australia renewed their vows according to these Constitutions.

Bishop Quinn had given instructions to Sister Clare Wright regarding the Chapter and warned her that unless she did as he wished she was not to return to Queensland. When Mary finally met him in April 1875, he attempted to prevent her from visiting the sisters. In spite of this, Mary, confident in her authority as the elected Mother General, visited each of the communities, thoroughly explained the Constitutions and the changes that had been made to the original Rule. After this the sisters in Queensland renewed their vows according to these Constitutions. Before Mary left Queensland in June another meeting with Bishop Quinn came to a compromise of sorts. He accepted Sister Josephine McMullen as the new Provincial but on sufferance. In return, Mary agreed to leave the sisters in Queensland until he was able to find other sisters to replace them in the schools. He thought that, in the meantime, he could influence the authorities in Rome to make the sisters become a diocesan group.

To achieve his end, Bishop Quinn worked on the weaknesses of Father Woods who grieved over the changes made to his Rule especially that regarding poverty. From 1876 onwards he took every opportunity to try to convince the sisters to accept Bishop Quinn's proposal to become a diocesan Congregation.

Mary paid a visit to Brisbane in April 1878 and remained there for more than three months. She returned in late November only to find that some of the sisters had been secretly meeting and communicating with Father Woods and were preparing to join him. However Mary was able to convince them of their obligations. She was back again in April 1879 and this time remained there until the end of the year. During these visits she met with the Bishop and tried to come to an agreement about the Constitutions and Central Government. He was adamant that he did not accept her authority and, when negotiations with him failed, Mary withdrew all the sisters from the Queensland schools except those at Bowen and Bundaberg which were to remain open until the Bishop had other religious to replace them.

In early December, Mary, taking Sister Josephine Carolan with her, went to Sydney to meet with Archbishop Vaughan who assured her that he would accept the sisters into his Archdiocese and warmly upheld the Constitutions accepting Central Government and her role as Mother General. Bishop Torreggiani of Armidale agreed to do likewise and begged for sisters. Mary organised accommodation for them and returned to Brisbane.

The people of Brisbane, where the sisters had been teaching, found out that they were leaving and they petitioned the Bishop to allow them to stay, but to no avail. Finding out that the sisters were to leave on Tuesday, 16 December 1879, they quickly organised functions to raise funds for them. An address read to the sisters at the convent on the day of departure and reported in the *Brisbane Courier* on 17 December 1879 read in part:

> The time at our disposal was short, but the enthusiasm which responded to our appeals was so great that in one week we were able to dispose of all the tickets for a raffle, with a net result of over £150. Some musical well-wishers inaugurated a concert ... after this we made a collection which, notwithstanding the two previous appeals to the public in the raffle and concert, realised in a few days £129 18s ... it will be seen that a sum of £309 18s has been obtained in a few weeks.[1]

The report went on to say that the Superioress, Mother Mary MacKillop, rose to reply but was overcome and shed tears which were echoed by all those present. The people then accompanied the sisters from the convent to the wharf

> when a second farewell, almost as affecting as was that at the convent took place, and if prayers and blessings and vows of kindly remembrance can do the Sisters of St Joseph good they bore many a one with them yesterday.[2]

For the most part the sisters left with few belongings and sailed into their new life in Sydney.

It was thus that Mary arrived in New South Wales leaving behind the memory of a hard-fought battle for the Constitutions and the right for Central Government against the powerful Bishop of Brisbane. Unable to reach any compromise, Mary accepted the protection of Archbishop Roger Vaughan of Sydney finding in him and his Vicar General staunch supporters and some solace for her truly broken heart. At the same time, Mary carried the very painful memory that Father Woods, her beloved Father Founder, had sided with Bishop Quinn and had attempted to lure some of the sisters to be the founding members of a diocesan group. A few agreed to this, as did some ex-sisters, and these were installed at Bundaberg in July 1880. As the Sisters of Saint Joseph moved out of Bundaberg, Mackay and Bowen other ex-sisters, including Sister Clare Wright, were installed by Father Woods. The experiment was not successful and although recruits came and went as did the ex-sisters, the diocesan sisters gradually dispersed.[3]

---

1. *Brisbane Courier,* 17 December 1879, 5.
2. *Brisbane Courier,* 17 December 1879, 5.
3. Margaret McKenna, *With Grateful Hearts! Mary MacKillop and the Sisters of St Joseph in Queensland, 1970–1970* (North Sydney: Sisters of St Joseph, 2009), 165

Bishop Quinn was dead by August 1881, just over twelve short months after the departure of Mary and the sisters. Then Father Woods left Queensland for an Asian Expedition in August 1882. By 1897 the diocesan group had ceased to exist.

Bishop Torreggiani's request for sisters for his Diocese of Armidale was an added relief for Mary in that she would not have to find the money to transport any members of the large group back to Adelaide. She saw the providence and guiding hand of her good God in all of this and her acceptance of God's will was to bear fruit in the years to come.

When Mary and her sisters arrived in Sydney, her relatives, the McNabs, 'all goodness and kindness' as she told her mother, had organised a house at 153 Forbes Street Woolloomooloo as accommodation for them.[4] Here they settled and she wasted no time in requesting her friends, the Jesuits, to allow Father Bixio to give them a Retreat before Christmas. After the traumas of the previous years, times of spiritual rest and renewal were sorely needed. Then, spiritually fortified, Mary and the sisters were ready to begin their ministry in New South Wales.

---

4. Mary MacKillop to her mother, 2 January 1880.

Chapter Two
1880, A Year of Foundations

After Christmas the sisters were prepared to move into the schools that the Vicar General had chosen for them. The first of these was Penrith. To Bishop Reynolds in Adelaide, Mary had written in December 1879':

> that it is decided that our first foundation is to be at Penrith, 34 miles out of Sydney ... the Vicar General is taking us up to see a suitable house for the convent.[1]

She wrote telling her mother that

> The Vicar General, too, has warmly taken up our cause and was kind enough to take us 30 miles yesterday to see about necessary arrangements for our new convent here.[2]

No elaboration of details of the 'new convent' was given but it was merely a cottage and the school no more than a stable in the yard of the presbytery. Sisters Baptista Molloy, Benedict Ahern, Margaret Crowe and Alphonsus Kennedy formed this first community. All four sisters had entered in Queensland in 1873.

Mary had also told her mother that she was anxious to get home to Kensington, South Australia, as soon as possible, but first she wanted to see to this new beginning at Penrith and, besides, she thought more sisters would come from Queensland before she left. Indeed, the *Telegraph* newspaper could report on 10 January 1880 that

---

1. Mary MacKillop to Bishop Reynolds, 27 December 1879.
2. Mary MacKillop to her mother, Flora MacKillop, 2 January 1880.

> five of them [Sisters of St Joseph] from Mackay arrived in Brisbane yesterday morning by the Victoria, s.s, and will leave this evening by the same vessel for Sydney. There are four still remaining at Mackay in charge of the orphanage, and they will continue their duties there until relieved by the Sisters of Mercy.³

In spite of the fact that five more sisters had arrived from Queensland, no one had time to sit idle as more requests for sisters came in. With the passing of the Public Instruction Act of 1880 and the withdrawal of grants to non-denominational schools, the Sisters of St Joseph were heaven sent for Archbishop Vaughan, his Vicar General and the priests who would otherwise have to find money to pay the teachers in the denominational schools.

The Parish priest of Penrith, Father Phelan, wanted sisters at South Creek and was able to get a cottage there as well. The sisters chosen to open South Creek were Sisters Patrick Barry and Rose Lehane both of whom had entered in Brisbane in 1873. In July, Father Phelan was able to write to Mary that the work of Sisters Baptista, Benedict, Margaret and Alphonsus had the schools in a 'flourishing condition . . . the school room looks well now inside—new desks, new forms . . . all from the proceeds of the children's concert.'⁴

What amazing women these were, who in the space of a few months were able to prepare the children for a concert. Their fun draising activities were not restricted to concerts. Bazaars were also organised within a short time. One such was reported in the *Freeman's Journal* on 19 November 1881. It was in aid of St Joseph's Convent at Penrith but the sisters at South Creek made their contributions with beautiful handwork as did the children of the South Creek school who provided beautiful cushions.⁵ The sisters assisted each other in these fundraisers.

---

3. *The Telegraph*, 10 January 1880, 2.
4. Father Phelan to Mary MacKillop, 27 July 1889. South Creek is now known as St Marys.
5. *Freeman's Journal,* 19 November 1881, 15.

St Joseph's Convent Penrith NSW.

By July 1882 alterations and additions to the convent at Penrith were almost completed and in an edition of the *Freeman's Journal* at this time there appeared a reference to the convent at South Creek. It stated:

> Mr Alcock of South Creek we are informed, has made a present to the Sisters there of a valuable cottage and garden, besides having given them a house rent free since their arrival at South Creek.[6]

Years later, at the blessing and opening of a new convent at Penrith in 1906, mention was made by Father Barlow, the Parish priest, that when the Sisters of St Joseph came to open a school in Penrith in 1880 'the accommodation was very meagre to teach in, as an old slab stable was substituted for a school, then situated in the yard of the Presbytery'.[7]

Cardinal Moran who was present on that occasion recalled that when he visited South Creek soon after he came to Australia in September 1884, he found

---

6. *Freeman's Journal*, 15 July 1882, *16*.
7. *Nepean Times*, 10 November 1906, 7.

> the Sisters located in a place that looked like a wayside shanty. On asking why they resided in such a place he was told that no other could be found.[8]

The 'valuable cottage' given by Mr Alcock did not measure up to the standards expected by the Cardinal but if the newspaper can be believed the sisters would have been grateful to be given a gift of house and garden.

Such were the conditions that the sisters joyfully accepted in those early years of the 1880s but once settled they made haste to improve matters, notably by arranging concerts that provided the finance for improvements. It seemed that at first the improvements were for the schools not the convents. Concerts featured in each new foundation and were reported in great detail in the newspapers of the day.

When Sisters Eulalia McDermott, Claver Dooley and Angela D'Arcy opened a school at Lithgow in February 1880 the parish priest was Father Garvey. They arrived a short time before St Patrick's Church, Lithgow was blessed and opened by Archbishop Vaughan on 22 February 1880. On this occasion he spoke of

> the Sisters of St Joseph who had just come to the district, and said that if nature and light and colour were beautiful, there was something more touching and more beautiful still, and that was the picture of those who had, through love of God and of souls, dedicated themselves in the habit of holy religion in the service of the rich and the poor, and to the instruction of little children.[9]

The Archbishop was asked to open the school which was to be in the church until a school was built. He expressed his pleasure in being able to introduce the sisters to the people of Lithgow. Fifty children were enrolled on that day and school commenced. Mary was not mentioned but she was, no doubt, present.

---

8. *Nepean Times*, 10 November 1906, 7.
9. *Freeman's Journal*, 22 February 1880, 14.

St Joseph's Convent Lithgow NSW.

At this time a foundation was made at Wallerawang about ten miles from Lithgow. Mary's letter to Sisters Bridget Kellegher and Martina O'Neill, both of whom had entered in Brisbane in 1874, contained the message that she hoped that they had warm clothes and blankets. She charged them with telling her everything when they wrote. Mary took delight in hearing every little piece of news of the sisters in each place. She did not forget the friends of the sisters and in her letter asked them to

> remember me kindly to the Lonergans. I am grateful to them for their constant kindness. Pray for me dear Sister Bridget. How do you like New South Wales? [10]

Mary had obviously met the Lonergans of Wallerawang and so wished to express her gratitude to them for their kindness to the sisters. Wherever Mary went she made contacts with the people and she never forgot these friends.

Seeing the poverty around the slum areas of Sydney, Mary, with the support of Archbishop Vaughan, had the satisfaction of seeing a

---

10. Mary MacKillop to the sisters at Wallerawang, 28 November 1880.

Providence set up in Gloucester Street in The Rocks area where the sisters opened a house on 6 March 1880. Sisters Josephine Carolan and Ignatius Griffin who had come with Mary from Brisbane were chosen to begin the work.[11]

In March 1880, Father Athy, a Benedictine, welcomed the sisters to Cooranbong. Sister Collette Carolan was one of the pioneer sisters. Writing from Dapto to Mary, Sister Bonaventure Mahony mentioned that she had received a letter from Sister Collette who requested a teacher for Cooranbong who would not require a large salary.[12]

The sisters were not unmindful of the lay teachers whose places they were taking when state aid was withdrawn from the denominational schools, and parishes were unable to afford to pay these teachers, hence Sister Collette's request.

In May 1881 The *Freeman's Journal* reported that

> our sequestered town of Cooranbong was the scene of more than usual religious demonstration on Sunday last the Feast of the patronage of St. Joseph, Patron of the Universal Church. Twenty-six of the children attending the school conducted by the Sisters of St Joseph made their first Communion . . . attired simply and gracefully in white dress and veil . . . The good Sisters of St Joseph had a dejeunee prepared . . . The Sisters have eighty children in attendance.[13]

The fact that all the children who made their first communion were dressed in white dresses suggests that this was a girls' school. This is confirmed when the Cooranbong School had its concerts reported in detail in the local papers of the day and the one reported in the *Newcastle Herald* in June 1887 mentioned an interesting fact that the performers were all girls.[14]

A new two-storey convent was built for the sisters in 1892 and was blessed and opened by Cardinal Moran on 5 November of that year in the presence of a large number of parishioners.[15] Mary was in

---

11. The Providence was a place that relied for its income on gifts and donations for its livelihood and that of the residents.
12. Sister Bonaventure Mahony to Mary MacKillop, 15 May 1880.
13. *Freeman's Journal*, 21 May 1881, 9.
14. *Newcastle Morning Herald and Miners' Advocate*, 30 June 1887, 9.
15. *Freeman's Journal*, 12 November 1892, 15.

Sydney at this time so she was probably there, although there is no record of her presence.

Before Mary left Sydney in mid–March 1880, other foundations were being negotiated. Tenterfield, Dapto, Inverell and Picton were to follow in that first year. No doubt Mary visited some of these places before she sent her sisters to open them. Before her return to Kensington, South Australia, she appointed Sister Bonaventure as Provincial and she it was who kept Mary informed of the progress of the new foundations of that year.

Sister Bonaventure Mahony. Image from Kathleen E. Burford rsj. (1991) *Unfurrowed Fields* p.38. Unattributed SOSJ image, original not found.

Knowing that the sisters were now in the safe hands of Archbishop Vaughan and his priests, Mary set out on the long journey to Adelaide, and arrived at Kensington on the 19 March 1880, St Joseph's night. After a few days of illness Mary wrote a joint letter to Sisters

Bonaventure and Josephine in which she said that she was 'anxious to hear from each of you to know how each school is getting on and how you, my dear children, are—each individually'.

She was anxious to hear how the sisters were progressing in the new schools and concluded her letter with a blessing for all:

> May God bless you one and all. I shall send this first to the Providence, for I do not know whether Sister Provincial is there or at Lithgow. If she is not at the Providence S.M. Josephine Carolan can take a copy to send to Cooranbong and Tenterfield and forward this to the Provincial who will send copies to the other houses.[16]

No general comment about the sisters was good enough for Mary. She required an account of each individual sister and each individual school. She wanted to know how many children were on the roll, what school fees were being paid and, of course, she would be delighted if the sisters told any funny little incident that they knew would bring a hearty laugh from their Mother General.

On Good Friday, 26 March 1880, Sisters Gonzaga Kennedy, Justina Lupton and a postulant, Cyril Doran, arrived direct from Queensland to open the convent and school at Tenterfield.[17] The Superior was Sister Gonzaga who lost no time in writing to Mary telling of their grand house which had mirrors in each room. She wrote that they

> arrived here on Good Friday. I did not feel the least tired but Sisters Justina and Cyril did. We commenced work on Holy Saturday. We had to prepare the children for Confirmation and First Communion as the Bishop was expected in a fortnight. We had to work hard to instruct them as they know very little of their catechism. The Bishop confirmed nearly 50 persons on last Sunday and was pleased with the order of the children.[18]

---

16. Mary MacKillop to Sisters Bonaventure and Josephine, 27 March 1880.
17. Sister Cyril Doran was a postulant who entered in Brisbane in December 1879. Later on she changed her name to Sister Camilla.
18. Sister Gonzaga Kennedy to Mary MacKillop, 17 April 1880.

St Joseph's Convent Tenterfield NSW.

As the Sisters of St Joseph did not teach music at this time, they employed a Miss Pierce to teach music and form a choir. In newspaper accounts of those early days, concerts were given much space in the local papers and invariably, mention by name was made of the music teacher who helped organise the concert and acted as accompanist. At various times Annie MacKillop and Uncle Donald McDonald's daughters, particularly Flora and Maggie, were called upon to fill the role of music teacher at various schools.[19]

Father Petre at Dapto vacated his house at West Dapto for Sisters Aloysius Lenihan, Eulalia McDermott and a Postulant, Mary Ann Christie. They were accompanied by the Provincial, Sister Bonaventure, when they arrived at West Dapto on 14 May 1880. School was taught in one of the large upstairs rooms of the former presbytery. Lively letters went from the sisters to Mother Mary telling of their kind pastor, Father Petre, who was so impressed with the sisters and their work that he was soon begging for two more sisters to start a school at nearby Albion Park. Sister Mary Ann did the cooking,

---

19. Mary MacKillop and Father Woods did not approve of the teaching of instrumental music. Mary felt that lessons in music would give poor children ideas totally opposed to their position in life. As a number of parents in New South Wales were asking for music lessons, Mary compromised by allowing the sisters to engage suitably qualified women as music teachers.

milked the cows, and made the butter which was sold by the sisters for five pence per pound. This was needed to supplement their meagre school fees as money was always short in country places.[20]

St Joseph's School West Dapto NSW. c.1898. Used with permission.

Picton was given special consideration as the priest, Dean Hanley, was aged and in ill health, and so the sisters arrived there at the end of May 1880. Mary brought Sister Veronica Champion from South Australia to be the leader of this community. She had entered in Adelaide in October 1871 at the height of the time of the excommunication. Veronica became a very valuable member of the young congregation. She wrote to Mother Mary on 15 June 1880 to tell her that

> the people are in a very backward state as regards religion . . . no Catholic School here for the past 12 years . . . 30 children on roll . . . at first we were in two rooms at the hotel, now we're in a rented house (12/- per week).[21]

A new convent was blessed and opened by Archbishop Vaughan on 15 January 1882.[22]

---

20. Bernadette O'Sullivan, *Nothing without God: The Story of a Hundred Years, Dapto 1880–1980* (Kiama. Weston & Co, Publisher, 1980), 22.
21. Sister Veronica Champion to Mary MacKillop, 15 June 1880.
22. *Freeman's Journal*, 7 January 1882, 15.

St Joseph's Convent Picton NSW.

Sister Veronica Champion.

Although at least thirty-five sisters had come from Queensland, Sister Bonaventure made a request to Mary for more sisters from Adelaide. Her reply on 10 June 1880 stated the case very firmly when she wrote that

> you ask me to send some more Sisters—I cannot. I cannot meet the wants here and already there is great dissatisfaction amongst the priests who have accused me of sending Sisters to N.S.W. who were required here. I grieve to say that I can scarcely keep my temper with some of them, they are so selfish, so unlike the generous ones you meet in New South Wales.[23]

These priests felt that they had a point. They needed the sisters for their schools and Mary was sending some of their best teachers to New South Wales. Sister Bonaventure was running out of sisters! However she obviously made some other arrangements as the foundations went ahead.

Bishop Torreggiani was anxious for a foundation at Inverell. On 11 June, accompanied by the Provincial, Sisters Lucy O'Neill and Philomena Hyland arrived with their Superior, Sister Casimir Meskill, whom Mary had sent from Adelaide.[24] Sister Casimir described the convent and school prepared by Father Cherubini as being

> two houses, four rooms in one and five in the other, two of which are large enough for the school; the other three can be fitted up for boarders, as many are expected.[25]

This was one place where the sisters did not have to live in a cottage that looked like a wayside shanty. Bishop Torreggiani wanted the best he could afford for the sisters.

Mary's next letter to Sisters Bonaventure and Josephine on 18 May 1880 expressed her pleasure about the sisters managing to open Inverell.[26] She was grateful to Bishop Torreggiani for his care of the sisters and the welcome he gave them in his Diocese so had been anxious to accede to his request for sisters. Annie MacKillop wrote in a letter to her sister Mary on 16 June 1880 that Sister Bonaventure had 'left for Armidale on Tuesday . . . and will be away for five weeks'.[27]

---

23. Mary MacKillop to Sister Bonaventure Mahony, 10 June 1880.
24. This sister could have been either Philomena O'Neill or Philomena Hyland.
25. Sister Bonaventure to Mary MacKillop, 13 June 1880.
26. Mary MacKillop to Sisters Bonaventure and Josephine, 18 May 1880.
27. Annie MacKillop to Mary MacKillop, 16 June 1880.

This meant that Sister Bonaventure was making long stops at Tenterfield and Inverell, companioning the sisters in these distant places and seeing to their welfare.

Sister Casimir Meskill.

The House of Providence in Gloucester Street soon outgrew the number of guests resident there so the enterprising Sister Josephine moved her family to a rented property in 79 Kent Street near St Bridget's Church and the Hall. The house was home to twelve sisters, ten postulants, twenty-two children and fourteen adults and, as if that was not enough for their zeal, they supported three families.[28]

The Providence, The Rocks NSW.

---

28. Sister Josephine Carolan to Mary MacKillop, 19 August 1880.

In July 1880, the sisters at Bundaberg were replaced by the new diocesan sisters and Sister Teresa Maginess and her companions arrived in Sydney and stayed at the Providence until they too were sent out to swell the numbers in the new foundations.

With sisters now resident in Kent Street, the Marist Fathers asked for sisters to take over the denominational school known as St Bridget's Girls' School at 107 Kent Street and this they did on 2 August 1880. The *Freeman's Journal* reported on 7 August that

> St Bridget's Girls' School has been withdrawn from the control of the Government and placed under the management of the Sisters of St. Joseph . . . On Monday last the Sisters were installed in the school and they at once entered upon their duties.[29]

When the year 1880 came to a close, Mary could look back with relief and gratitude to God for the rapid spread of the sisters in New South Wales and for the energy and zeal with which they settled into their new homes, poor though they were, but knowing that they had the support of their priests and people who were poor too. The success of the Providence in the slum area of The Rocks that provided a home for the postulants, the sisters and the destitute children and women gave Mary great joy.

---

29. *Freeman's Journal*, 7 August 1880, 14.

Chapter Three
Developments, 1881–1883

Mary could see the need for a Novitiate in Sydney as did Archbishop Vaughan.[1] In her discussions with him she informed him that a second Novitiate could only be opened with the permission of the Holy See. The Bishop lost no time in negotiating with Rome and in March 1881, he sent Mary a copy of the permission he had received from the Holy See but he left the carrying out of this permission to the sisters. Mary saw that a Novitiate in Sydney would allow her to accept the many young women who were coming forward for admittance to the congregation. Paul Gardiner sj noted in his biography of Mary MacKillop that

> there would be long term advantages to the Church in the educational struggle if the Josephites had a centre in Sydney. This would also help to untangle the confusion caused by the existence of the Bathurst community bearing the same name and wearing the same habit as the Mother House Sisters. A Sydney novitiate would make the distinction clear and candidates would know what they were joining.[2]

The cost of sending women to Adelaide for their Novitiate was more than Mary could afford. When she returned to Sydney at the beginning of 1881 she visited the convents and schools already opened throughout the state. These were scattered, and it is not known whether she visited all of them, Tenterfield and Inverell being so far from Sydney.

---

1. A Novitiate is a house where Novices of a Congregation live and are trained.
2. Paul Gardiner sj, *Mary MacKillop, An Extraordinary Australian* (Sydney: EJ Dwyer, 1994), 253.

Mary visited Lithgow in early February and whilst there she travelled to Terra Bella the home of Uncle Duncan MacKillop's family.[3] Writing from the Providence, then at 79 Kent Street, to a Cameron cousin she told him that she had 'lost his address and only obtained it last week from a Glengary man called Ferguson, whom I met up at Terra Bella.'[4] Her reason for writing to him was revealed towards the end of her letter:

> I am sending you a collecting card for our House here. The Archbishop is so good to us and has been a kind friend to me. I wish you could put something, too, for my own especial house in Adelaide upon which all these branch houses have so much to depend. If you answer this letter soon do so to my present address where it will find me, but in a few weeks I shall be returning to Adelaide.[5]

Mary used every opportunity to canvass among her relations for donations for the works of the sisters and this is one such example. She also took every opportunity to visit relations, this time the family of her father's brother, Duncan.

We do know that she visited Dapto as a letter from Sister Aloysius to Sister Bonaventure, dated 22 February 1881 stated:

> I am very anxious to hear how you and Mother got on after leaving here. I suppose that poor Mother was very ill, but I hope that the nice cool night air took it all away, but I fear it made you worse.[6]

At that time she also visited the newly opened convent and school at Bulli. This new church/school had been blessed and opened by Archbishop Vaughan the previous July.[7] The first Superior at Bulli was Sister Colette Carolan who had entered the convent in Brisbane during Mary's time there.

---

3. Uncle Duncan MacKillop was Alexander MacKillop's younger brother. He died in 1877 but his widow, Ann, was still alive at this time.
4. Mary MacKillop to a Cameron cousin, 14 February 1881.
5. Mary MacKillop to a Cameron cousin, 14 February 1881.
6. Sister Aloysius Lenihan to Sister Bonaventure, 22 February 1881.
7. A church/school was one which was set up by the sisters and pupils on Friday afternoon for Sunday Mass and then, on Monday, set up with desks for school on weekdays. During this era this was the pattern in many places in both South Australia and New South Wales.

St Joseph's Bulli NSW.

One business matter of great importance was to consent to Sister Josephine's wish to purchase a larger residence for the Providence. The place chosen was 'Cheshunt' at 3 Cumberland Street. This was a three-storey building with a large basement and once acquired would house the growing number of novices and postulants, as well as the other guests. Sister Josephine was not one to waste time and with a loan from the bank, the building was theirs by May 1881, by which time Mary had returned to Adelaide. The Providence was to become the Provincial House for the Sydney Archdiocese until the Mother House was moved to North Sydney in 1888.[8]

Mary had been anxious to return to the Mother House in Adelaide because she had to prepare for the Second General Chapter which was duly held in July 1881.[9] She was re-elected Mother General and Sister Bernard Walsh was appointed as Provincial of New South Wales. The matter of the second novitiate in Sydney was discussed and the result

---

8. A Provincial House was the main house in a Province (a group of Convents in a particular area).
9. A General Chapter is a meeting of the sisters held every six years. Delegates from each Province attend and it is a time for the election of the Mother General and her Council.

of interventions by Bishop Reynolds and Father Tappeiner, both of whom were not in favour of the Sydney Novitiate, was that it was to be deferred for the time being. However, Mary and her Councillors were given permission to go ahead should it be seen to be necessary. Mary was disappointed at this outcome but accepted the decision of the Chapter delegates.

The appointment of a new Provincial, Sister Bernard Walsh, for New South Wales left Sister Bonaventure free to take over the denominational school at Camperdown in October 1881. She had agreed to this foundation before leaving for the General Chapter. She, with two sisters and a lay teacher, walked daily from the Providence to Camperdown until a cottage was available for them. The parish priest held a meeting in March 1882, and reported on it in the *Freeman's Journal* of 1 April 1882.[10] At this meeting he proposed to build a church/school and a residence for the sisters. A church/school was opened in August 1882 but there was no mention at that time of a convent.[11] It is likely that the sisters provided themselves with a house at Camperdown.

St Joseph's School Camperdown NSW.

---

10. *Freeman's Journal*, 1 April 1882, 16.
11. *Freeman's Journal*, 19 August 1882, 18.

In December 1881, Mary wrote to Sister Bernard telling her that no more sisters would go from Adelaide unless their fares were paid. Sister Bernard was warned not to open any convents unless these conditions were adhered to.

Father Petre at Albion Park had been pleading for sisters for some time and, in preparation he formed a committee in 1881 to erect a convent and school. He wrote to Mary on 1 October 1881 telling of the progress of the proposed buildings:

> I have laid (or at least Fr. Mahoney has done so), the foundation of a convent and school here at Albion Park. The convent will have five rooms, two large, and three small. The school room will be about two yards away... the whole length of the building will be 30 ft.

He told her that there would be at least forty pupils and a large number of music pupils.[12] When he met Mary on her visit to Dapto he had been charmed by her and wrote numerous letters begging her to come back to visit them. He even bought a cedar bed for her comfort should she come there!

St Joseph's Albion Park NSW. c.1906.

In her Christmas letter to the sisters in December 1881, Mary could look back on the previous years of uncertainty and trouble and write 'how good God has been to us bringing us from uncertainty and many troubles to the peace and security we have in N.S.W'.[13]

---

12. Father A W Petre to Mary MacKillop, 1 October 1881.
13. Mary MacKillop to the Sisters, 19 December 1881.

The death of Father Tappeiner sj in February 1882 caused deep sorrow to Mary and the sisters. He had been their kind and treasured friend and counsellor and was sorely missed by all.

The year 1882 saw the sisters begin teaching at Albion Park. A report in *The Wollongong Argus* of 13 July 1882, reported the transfer of Father Petre to the Hartley and Lithgow Mission and in part mentioned that

> his labours in the cause of education have been incessant. Besides having primarily established the convent schools of Dapto and Albion Park, both of which are in successful operation, he held classes for youth in various parts of the district.[14]

So it proved Father Petre was not to enjoy the benefits of his new presbytery, convent and school at Albion Park after labouring so long for their establishment. Mary met him later at Moss Vale and again when she visited Lithgow.

Years later another parish priest at Albion Park, Father W Hayden, wrote to Sister La Merci Mahony, asking that the same sisters be sent back to Albion Park and Dapto for the year 1905 because

> Sisters Edna [Purcell] and Placid [McMahon] are making a reformation in Dapto school, and Sisters Raphael [Gerock] and Gabrielle [Jordan] are doing equally well here . . . With Kind Regards to Mother Mary and self.[15]

When Government aid was withdrawn in 1882 from St John's School at 420 Kent Street, Archbishop Vaughan requested sisters for this school. In 1927 when the school was closing because of changes in the city's demography and the necessity for the church or school having passed, the writer of an article in *The Catholic Press* recalled the early days and reported that

> when the school was opened it was found that three Sisters were sufficient to cope with the needs of their new centre, only 20 children attending during the first few weeks . . . Within 12 months of the founding of the school, however, the regular attendance of children numbered over 100 a day . . . In those days the good Sisters attended not only to the mental needs of the children under their care, but also to their physical wants.

---

14. *Wollongong Argus*, 13 July 1882, 2.
15. Father W. Hayden to Sister La Merci, 27 December 1904.

> Every child attending St John's Poor School was given two meals each day, thanks to the charity of many public spirited men and women.[16]

Breakfast and lunch were provided and a sister cooked a meal for the children after having collected meat and vegetables from shops along the route from the Providence to the school. As well, the sisters visited the sick, the poor and the afflicted.

Sister Gertrude O'Gorman was in charge of St John's Poor School for many years and mention was made of her in an article in the *Freeman's Journal* of 18 June 1908.[17] The writer of this article encouraged people to help her in her work for these little ones by donating money, clothes and groceries to her at the school. Again, her work was eulogised in an article on 8 September 1921:

> Sister Mary Gertrude has been in charge of St. John's for many years. She knows every child who comes to her for care and comfort, every mother who finds the burdens of life so heavy that she cannot carry them unassisted. She has a heart big enough to take in a whole city of such sufferers and to sympathise with them. At the present time there are over 100 children attending St John's Poor School. There they are fed, clothed and educated.[18]

Such was the ministry of the early pioneer sisters in New South Wales, not only at St John's Poor School, but wherever they established themselves whether in the poorest areas of the city of Sydney or in the distant rural villages.

Annandale school was opened in 1882 when there was a house at Camperdown. The Annandale sisters lived there and walked daily to a small terrace house in Johnston Street. Later Mary was able to rent a house for them. Here they resided and taught school.

Years later when a larger house was needed, Mary recorded in her diary that on 5 July 1899, she had sent Sister Josephine with Sister Stanislaus Mulrooney to rent a house in Annandale and purchase furniture for it. On the following day she went to see the new convent/ school for herself. Then she saw the Cardinal about the house and he

---

16. *The Catholic Press*, 22 September 1927, 19.
17. *Freeman's Journal*, 18 June 1908, 23.
18. *Freeman's Journal*, 8 September 1921, 3.

consented to give it three months' trial. Next day she saw the sisters settled in their new home. No time wasted![19]

Mary left Adelaide in December 1882 bound for Sydney. She broke her journey in Melbourne and was able to visit her sister Lexie who was dying at the Good Shepherd Convent in Abbotsford. Flora and Annie were there, too, to be with Lexie in her last days but Mary was in Sydney when word came of Lexie's death on 31 December 1882. Flora accepted this death with patience and resignation but when Mary wrote to her brother, Donald, she encouraged him to write often to their mother reminding him that 'there are only three now left out of eight'.[20]

Mary was ill at the Providence for two weeks in early January 1883. When she recovered her time was taken up in visiting the sisters and discussing with the Provincial, Sister Bernard, the new foundations that were scheduled for that year and probably visiting some of them: Camden, Villa Maria, Jamberoo, and St Brigid's Boys' School.

One of the problems with which she had to deal regarded the land on which St Michael's Church, Cumberland Street, was built. This church had been built by the Marist Fathers on an unused part of the Providence land owned by the Sisters of St Joseph. John Hosie in his book about the Marists in colonial Australia tells the story of the Marist, Father Joly, and his role in the building of St Michael's:

> On the land owned by the Marists, there was no suitable position on which a church could be built. But their new next door neighbours, the Sisters, had an unused corner of their land which would be ideal . . . he came to the surprising arrangement with the Sisters, through their superiors, that the Marists would build a church at their own expense, on the land owned by the Sisters . . . only at the insistence of the Foundress of the Sisters of St Joseph, Mother Mary MacKillop does it appear that any agreement relating to ownership was reached. It was to the effect that if either wished to leave, that party would relinquish title and both land and church would go to the party which remained. More methodical in this instance than Joly, MacKillop requested that the unusual agreement be put in writing.[21]

---

19. Mary MacKillop's Diary, 5 July 1899.
20. Mary MacKillop to Donald MacKillop, 26 January 1883.
21. John Hosie, *Challenge: The Marists in Colonial Australia* (Sydney: Allen & Unwin 1987), 247.

The document was duly drawn up and signed by Father Joly and Mary and dated 28 April 1883 although the church had been completed and opened in October 1882. This is one instance of the many business affairs that Mary had to deal with in the time that she was in Sydney. One can only conjecture why this agreement had not been put in place before the church was built.

St Michael's Church, exterior and interior, 1882. Photos provided by Marist Fathers Provincial Archives.
Used with permission.

The convent at Camden was opened at the request of Father James Sheridan who, when the time came, soon had all in readiness for the sisters whose first convent was in Edward Street.[22] Tenders were called for a convent in October 1904 so the first one was a temporary residence.[23] Father Sheridan had also requested sisters for two other parts of his parish, The Oaks and Burragorang, but these convents were not opened for some years since Father Sheridan was moved from Camden parish before the sisters arrived there.

---

22. Burford, *Unfurrowed Fields*, 49.
23. *South Coast Times and Wollongong Argus*, 29 October 1904, 5.

St Joseph's Convent Camden NSW. c.1906.

The Marist Fathers requested sisters for their parish school at Villa Maria, Hunters Hill. When the sisters arrived in 1883 they lived in an old stone house owned by the Marist Fathers. From this base the sisters taught at three schools: Villa Maria School, St Charles' Ryde, and Woolwich. They walked to these schools each day. When the old stone house proved inadequate, the sisters moved into another one-storey wooden building on the corner of Gladesville Road and Mary Street, also built and owned by the Marist Fathers. Here they had room for boarders and a large room was available for a schoolroom. This convent was burned down in 1907 but, thanks to the alertness of a boarder, no lives were lost. In her diaries Mary recorded that she visited this convent at Villa Maria on many occasions during her time in New South Wales.

The village of Jamberoo welcomed the sisters in the year 1883. Sisters Eulalia McDermott, Columba O'Leary and Magdalen Mary Thompson formed the first community, and lived in a cottage near the church. Sister Eulalia wrote to Mary on 8 July 1884 telling her 'Frs Riorden and Hayes visited the school yesterday. Fr Hayes said he used to think Bulli the best school, but now he thinks Jamberoo the champion'.[24]

Jamberoo had a large population of Irish Catholics who settled in the fertile valley and raised large families. At the time of the opening of the school there were some ninety children in attendance. Having visited the sisters and worked with the Provincial, Sister Bernard and

---

24. Sister Eulalia to Mary MacKillop, 8 July 1884.

her councillors, Mary was ready to return to Adelaide towards the end of May 1883. Trouble was brewing there.

Shortly after her return she had to face the Commission set up by Bishop Reynolds and his Vicar General and this resulted in her being expelled from Adelaide in November 1883 and being illegally deposed as the Mother General.[25] With a heavy heart she set out from Adelaide on 17 November via Melbourne and took up residence at the Providence in Sydney.

In December she wrote to the sisters in South Australia a long letter in which she expressed her sorrow at the happenings in Adelaide and begged their prayers and pleaded with them to have patience and trust. She went on to write 'the beautiful sea breeze here has done me so much good, but I miss it and am not so well in the country.'[26]

Wanting to tell them about Sydney she continued with news that she had returned the previous day from a visit to Penrith where she was happy to report that the sisters had a fine convent free from debt. She had visited Camden and found there 'a little Paradise of quiet and order' as was Picton. She told of the offer from Dean Kenny of a house for a Novitiate and promise of financial assistance. In Sydney the debts did not weigh as heavily on her and the sisters as they had in Adelaide.[27] However, she was hiding from the sisters the true reason for her leaving Adelaide, that is, her expulsion by the Bishop. All this was a puzzle for Mary because the Bishop had once been her greatest friend and support. Time would reveal to her the underlying reasons for his actions.

In some instances, withdrawals from schools had to be made when school populations dwindled for various reasons. One of these was when railways bypassed once populated areas of the time or in mining areas where the rise and fall of the industry saw consequent changes in population. One such place that the sisters withdrew from in 1883 was the convent at Wallerawang.

---

25. This Commission, also referred to as the Apostolic Commission, was called by Bishop Reynolds to enquire into the life and finances of the sisters in his diocese. The sisters were made to take an oath never to reveal what occurred while they were interviewed. The Commission was a source of much disquiet for the sisters and for Mary herself. The so-called 'evidence' interpreted by some of the members of the Commission was the cause of Mary's expulsion from Adelaide by Bishop Reynolds.
26. Mary MacKillop to the South Australian sisters, 17 December 1883.
27. Mary MacKillop to the South Australian sisters, 17 December 1883.

On 7 January 1884 seven novices were professed in a ceremony at St Michael's Church, Lower Fort Street.[28] *The Freeman's Press* reported that this was

> the first of the kind in Sydney in connection with a religious community which has of late years taken up its habitation in our midst . . . the community of St Joseph, although not of many years' residence in Sydney, is yet too well known from its good works to need any further eulogy at our hands. And the addition of seven members to the order will have the effect of strengthening to a large extent the hands of the good Sisters in the efforts they are making to do good amongst God's poor.[29]

This was the first of many such ceremonies that would take place at St Michael's until there was a chapel at North Sydney large enough to accommodate those invited.

Sister Josephine Carolan and the group of sisters professed in 1884.

---

28. The novices professed were Sisters Mary of the Sacred Heart Cordner, Antonia Wilson, Magdalen Mary Thompson, Gabrielle Jordan, Charles Flanagan, Claude Turner and Cuthbert Duff.
29. *Freeman's Journal*, 12 January 1884, 15.

Bishop Torreggiani of Armidale had a completely furnished convent ready for the sisters at Glen Innes and suggested that the sisters come after Christmas when he would accompany them for the opening of the school.[30] On 15 January 1884 the Bishop and Sisters Magdalen, Agatha Doherty and Denis Malone arrived to open the school which they did on 21 January with about thirty pupils. Father Marianus, a Capuchin, was the parish priest at the time.

St Joseph's Convent Glen Innes NSW. c.1906.

Mary sent Sister Bernard to represent her at this opening at Glen Innes whilst she visited the sisters down the coast. This she recounted in a letter to her mother. The convents and schools 'down the coast' were at Bulli, Dapto, Albion Park and Jamberoo. She wrote:

> All the time I was down South, the priests were so good to us, driving us from one parish to another, and taking the greatest care of our comfort. A very beautiful convent is awaiting us at Moss Vale, but I don't know when we can spare Sisters for it.[31]

Mary did find some 'spare' sisters and Moss Vale convent and school were opened soon after by Sisters Colette Carolan and Gabrielle Jordan. Mary visited there in February.

---

30. Bishop Torreggiani to Mary MacKillop, 29 October 1883.
31. Mary MacKillop to her mother, 25 January 1884.

Moss Vale NSW. 2009.

She wrote to Sister Calasanctius on 6 March 1884 regarding the house for the novitiate:

> Dean Kenny is giving up his whole place to us as soon as we can take it. I think we shall do so, please God, on St Joseph's Day. It is a nice house, 11 rooms and so retired in situation, yet in one of the best positions on North Shore.[32] He leaves us his little oratory—marble altar and all required for use, also part of his house furniture. I wish I could quietly settle down in the little nook and get charge of the novices.[33]

Bouts of illness still plagued Mary but the good news that she received from Rome in March 1884 caused her much relief as she hastened to inform the sisters in Adelaide:

> God's ways are most mysterious. Letters have come for me today from Rome stating that no orders had been given from there about the Visitation—that no report of it had reached Rome up to (the) time of date, February 16th. In my letter it says—talking of the Bishop—'He received no special powers

---

32. Also called North Sydney.
33. Mary MacKillop to Sister Calasanctius, 6 March 1884.

from Propaganda to act in the matter. It is true that a Bishop has in certain cases the position of Delegate of the Holy See, but this never gives him power to remove the Superior of any Institute'.[34]

It was a relief to Mary to know that Rome was upholding the Sisters of St Joseph but her own sufferings at this time were heavy upon her as she had to bear with the calumnies about her that were being poured into the ears of the Bishop in Adelaide and other prelates and priests whom she had considered to be her friends. They were led to believe that she was a drunkard and a squanderer of the Congregation's money. The knowledge that some of her own sisters had been the cause of these accusations was a deep sorrow, but true to her nature she forgave them and excused them.

Whilst all this was simmering below the surface, she calmly went on with the business of the Congregation but to Sister Mechtilde Woods she revealed the sorrow she felt at the defamatory stories that were circulating about her in Adelaide when she wrote 'I don't care for any sorrow this causes me save that I feel as if death would certainly be preferable to returning to Adelaide'.[35]

Whilst Mary continued with the many calls on her time as leader of the Congregation, beneath the outward show, her heart, as she said, was crushed with sorrow. Already she had gone through the dreadful time of the excommunication and the painful events in Bathurst with Bishop Matthew Quinn and then the struggle for the sisters' rights in Queensland with Bishop James Quinn and the heart-breaking split with her beloved Father Founder, Father Woods, and the defection of some of the sisters.[36] Therefore, to have the unjust expulsion from Adelaide by her one-time staunchest ally, Bishop Reynolds, and the horror of being labelled an alcoholic and a squanderer of the monies of the Congregation, would have broken the spirit of a much weaker person. Mary managed to see it all as part of the mystery of God's plan for her even though she was deprived of the friendship of those prelates she held dear.

---

34. Mary MacKillop to the Adelaide sisters, 24 March 1884.
35. Mary MacKillop to Sister Mechtilde Woods, 16 April 1884.
36. Father Founder was the title given by Mary MacKillop to Father Julian Tenison Woods who was the co-founder of the Sisters of St Joseph of the Sacred Heart.

But the works of the Congregation had to go on, so Mary expressed her desperate need for sisters to be available for an Auckland Mission and with the agreement of the Vicar General of Sydney, Sister Ignatius was chosen with Sister Casimir from Bishop Torreggiani's Diocese to travel to Auckland, New Zealand.[37]

She saw again the pressing necessity for the second Novitiate to be established in Sydney and gave Father Bianchi her reasons when she wrote:

> One reason why we are anxious to have a second Novitiate here in the Archdiocese of Sydney is that we thus can receive many postulants who would otherwise go to Bathurst. Another is that we can be supported here, whilst in Adelaide only a few can be supported. Want of means is a sad drawback in Adelaide, but from year to year we had hoped that it would have been otherwise, so did not complain. We are a little anxious as to Dr Moran's [the new Bishop's] views regarding such a work as ours, but if they be anything like the late Archbishop's, a Novitiate in the Archdiocese will be sure to succeed, both spiritually and temporally.
>
> As matters now stand in Adelaide, we could not send any postulants over, so availed ourselves of the Holy Father's permission for a 2nd Novitiate, and of certain discretionary powers given at the 2nd General Chapter, and so gave the holy Habit to some who had been waiting here long over their time. I beg, Rev. Father, that you will give us your support in this, for I know that my enemies blame me for it.[38] We have every inducement for a Novitiate here, ease in obtaining subjects, and support for them, a suitable house given for the purpose by a charitable priest, and every spiritual facility. Meanwhile, I am taking charge of these novices myself, leaving to the Provincial here the management of her Province, and not being able to do any active duty in South Australia under existing circumstances.[39]

---

37. Mary MacKillop to Sister Calasanctius, 2 April 1884.
38. Rev. Father was Father Bianchi, the Dominican priest who had reviewed and rewritten the Josephites Constitutions in 1874.
39. Mary MacKillop to Father Bianchi, 16 April 1884.

Before Mary's expulsion from Adelaide she had been able to accompany postulants due for the novitiate there as she travelled backwards and forwards from Sydney to Adelaide in those years after 1880.

Mary's letters spoke for themselves of her occupations at this time as did the following to Sister Monica Phillips on 9 May 1884:

> I have been very busy since my last, first helping the Dean in moving into his other house and arranging his books, etc., and then moving our own things in here and getting matters into discipline and order. Thank God we succeeded well and things are in good working order. The place is beautifully retired; though near one of the chief streets, it is as quiet as if miles away from other people. We have no noise, bustle or excitement, have a nice little garden and paddock with high fences, and little birds singing around us, their singing and the ticking of the clocks being the only sounds except at recreation, and, of course, necessary talking during the exercises and at study. I have taken the entire charge of the novices myself.[40]

To her brother Donald she wrote that:

> There are here five novices, Sister Mary Veronica and myself. One novice has to go to school every day with Sister M Veronica. The Dean takes the greatest interest in the novices, and has promised to give us instruction on religious as well as secular subjects.[41]

Mary settled into the house at North Sydney, Alma Cottage, whilst Sister Bernard, the Provincial, continued to live at the Providence.

---

40. 'Recreation' was the time when the sisters met to converse and enjoy each other's company. Silence was observed at other times. Mary MacKillop to Sister Monica Phillips, 9 May 1884.
41. Mary MacKillop to Sister Monica Phillips, 9 May 1884.

Alma Cottage, Mount Street North Sydney NSW. 2016. Photo taken by Sandy Leaitua. Used with permission.

Another joy for Mary at this time was the news that her best loved uncle, Uncle Donald McDonald and his wife, Aunt Eliza, were moving from Penola to Sydney. Uncle Donald had failed in business and had suffered a stroke. They decided to make a new start and so they moved to Sydney. Donald and Eliza had been staunch supporters of Mary throughout the early years of the Congregation and she looked forward to being able to repay their many kindnesses to her. The McDonalds had eight children one of whom died in infancy. Now adults and with good positions the older ones were supporting their parents. Mary wrote to her brother Donald, who was studying overseas, to tell him that their uncle and aunt had come to Sydney and were living 'in a nice house overlooking the harbour and not far from this convent'.[42] The younger girls, Maggie and Lizzie lived with their parents.

---

42. Mary MacKillop to her brother, Donald, 1 October 1884.

Mary had the consolation of having her mother come to Sydney about the end of May. During this visit Flora spent time with her brother, Donald, and his wife and family. She visited in Sydney until the 18 November when Mary saw her off on the *Ly-ee-moon* en route to Melbourne. Mary suggested to her that she (Mary) would keep a diary and send it to Flora when she did not have time to write, thus keeping her mother informed of her movements. Flora, in turn, welcomed and cared for Sister Calasanctius when she came to Melbourne from Sydney a short time later, and saw her on board the ship sailing to Adelaide.[43] Since there was no community of the sisters in Melbourne, Flora carried out many such commissions for her daughter.

Mary had a great love for the bishops and priests especially those who had played positive roles in their story and never failed to recognise their anniversaries. This is one such example, a Spiritual Bouquet for Archbishop Moran from the sisters in New South Wales as described by Mary in a letter to the sisters, on 12 September 1884:

> We have prepared as a little presentation to the Archbishop a Spiritual Bouquet or offering of prayers to be said in each of our convents for him. Each convent is mentioned—in all, fifteen in the Archdiocese and four in Armidale. It is prettily got up and surrounded by a border of rose, thistle and shamrock, with flags in shield form of the Pope, Great Britain, Ireland and South Australia, New South Wales; also the fleur-de-lis for France.[44]

The fifteen convents then established in New South Wales were at Penrith, St Marys, Cooranbong, Dapto, Lithgow, Picton, The Providence in Sydney, Camperdown, Annandale, Bulli, Albion Park, Camden, Hunters Hill, Jamberoo, and the Novitiate at North Sydney. The four in Armidale Diocese were Tenterfield, Inverell, Glen Innes and Kempsey West.

These foundations were a formidable achievement in the space of less than four years since the sisters' arrival in New South Wales. Only to her closest friends did Mary reveal the intense suffering she was enduring at this time, as she wrote to Sister Monica:

---

43. Sister Calasanctius was on her way home to South Australia from New Zealand.
44. Mary MacKillop to the sisters, 12 September 1884.

> Sorrow at the insincerity and unfaithfulness of some I have loved is telling upon me, and I feel more unable than usual to meet my crosses, but when I am a day or two well, I gain heart again ... Dearest Sister, forgive me if I seem to speak bitterly. I am wounded to the heart, and not being well or able for this constant struggle, am so tempted to give up and seek a rest that up to this I have never got, either in the world or in religion. <u>Your unswerving</u> fidelity and that of a few more like you is about the only thing that makes me keep up. For very shame I cannot desert those who are so faithful in the dark hour.[45]

It was indeed one of Mary's darkest hours, one that she revealed only to her dearest and trusted friends. In addition she could tell Sister Monica that when Bishop Reynolds was in Sydney earlier he did not come to see her or the sisters. Evidently he could not face them.

Contrasted with the weight of her own sufferings is the tale of yet another opening, a strange one this time. It is best told in her own words:

> We had to open a convent at Kempsey. Dr Torreggiani had two years ago offered us that place together with three of the other best towns in his diocese. We could not accept so he had to try to get other nuns. He had arranged for Sisters of Mercy, the convent was ready, and a priest sent to Sydney to meet them, and he waiting in Kempsey for them, when the supposed Sisters of Mercy turned out to be <u>impostors</u>, could not be received, and the poor Bishop was left in the lurch and a great scandal threatening. He then telegraphed to us at any cost to spare him some.
>
> I had started for Glen Innes, and towards the end of the day's journey, on arriving at a station, was met by a telegraph messenger from Sister Bernard telling me of the Bishop's difficulty and request. I replied to meet it if she could. Sister M Josephine [McMullen] asked to go for the present, and went with Sister de Chantal [Murphy] and a postulant, and thus a grave scandal was prevented, and the <u>sham</u> Sisters of Mercy got off with a warning.

---

45. Mary MacKillop to Sister Monica Phillips, 26 September 1884.

On another matter, she was happy to tell Sister Monica that

> Bulli and South Creek, also Lithgow, are free from debt. £1,000 has been paid on the Property, and the quarterly Interest always met. All bills paid weekly, or at furthest monthly . . . No debt on the Novitiate . . . So Sydney money matters are not as they were in Adelaide.[46]

The month of November 1884, was a busy one for Mary as she visited St John's School in Kent Street, then helped Sister Bonaventure prepare the children for the school examination at Camperdown. On 12 December she became very ill and was ordered quiet and rest and for this she went to Camperdown and remained there for some days with a high fever. When she recovered she returned to North Shore. In her diary Mary regularly reported on her days of illness which were frequent. Against these she struggled and as soon as possible resumed her duties.

She was unable to attend the school presentation at St Bridget's school where Sister Veronica Champion taught and had to be content to hear about the pleasure the Archbishop expressed at the work done there. He was so pleased that he gave 'a handsome work box as a prize to the best girl at the girls' school, and told Sister M Veronica that she should get up a tea party for the Infants (about 190 or more) and send the bill to him'.[47]

Mary was well enough to go to the St John's School Display where everything went off well. It is interesting that the children were highly commended for their elocution. Priests and people gave high praise for the standard of the display. In the diary that was meant for her mother she went into great detail about all that was said by the priests who were present and told how delighted she was that her dear Uncle Donald and Aunt Eliza were there to hear and see all the compliments that the sisters received for their work with the children.

After the display Mary went to the Providence, had some dinner and started for Moss Vale where she arrived later that evening in an exhausted state. She told her mother in the diary that

---

46. Mary MacKillop to Sister Monica Phillips, 26 September 1884.
47. Mary MacKillop's Diary, 17 December 1884.

a buggy had to be got from the hotel to take me to the convent. It had been such a long journey after a hot and trying day, and I had no refreshment since leaving the Providence—but a good quiet night's rest awaited me.[48]

It was display day at Moss Vale and Mary had to give out the prizes because the two priests were unable to be there. She expressed delight at the progress made by the children as they had improved so much. Even though the sisters had only been at Moss Vale since early in 1884, she was able to assess the improvement. The next day was a delightful one for Mary as she described it in her diary:

> After a good night started with Sister M Collette in a nice buggy driven by Jack, Mr Hanrahan's servant— visited a number of places— and begged a lot of fowls and geese to bring home with me for Xmas, Jack quite enthusiastic and doing a good part of the begging.[49] Great fun on getting back to the convent when Sister M Gabrielle came to take a bundle from me, and first hearing a hiss, found her sleeve pulled by something which turned out to be a goose and which she nearly let fall in her terror.[50]

One can almost hear Mary's hearty chuckle at poor Sister Gabrielle's distress! She did enjoy a joke. So on the next day, she was taken driving again by the trusty Jack as she reports that

> in the afternoon Jack had taken us for another drive and we brought home a turkey, geese, chickens and a sucking pig, which I begged for the fun of taking it home with me and shocking our dear Sister M Patrick, also a lame rosella parrot for Uncle.[51]

She was already anticipating the fun she would have with poor Sister Patrick. Who was going to get poor piggy ready for the Christmas Dinner?

---

48. Mary MacKillop's Diary, 18 December 1884.
49. 'Begging' was the name given to the practice carried out from the earliest days of the Congregation when the sisters asked people for donations of food, goods or money to assist them in their many charitable works.
50. Mary MacKillop's Diary, 20 December 1884.
51. Mary MacKillop's Diary, 22 December 1884.

On Monday 22 December she wrote in her diary that she had

> started for Sydney accompanied by Sister M Eulalia and M Mary who had arrived from Jamberoo during the night. Some of the committee men saw our livestock booked and in the train. Got all safely over to North Shore, where there was great amusement over poor piggy.[52]

Imagine sisters travelling from Jamberoo and arriving at Moss Vale during the night! They probably travelled by coach up the winding Jamberoo Mountain road and then on to Moss Vale which would have been another way of getting to Sydney, rather than taking the train or boat from Wollongong.

Mary always enjoyed the humorous stories that the sisters told her either in person, or in their letters, for example, when Father Garvey died she told her mother that he was the priest who had once mistaken her for Sister Bonaventure and about which she had great fun.[53]

Mary attended the display and prize-giving at Camperdown on 23 December and wrote a very thorough description of the decorations in the school and the pleasure of the Archbishop who also attended, as did Father Younge and Dean Kenny. The decorations at the school were described in detail, one unusual one was that 'Swung up high on ropes were cages containing canaries (all brought by friends of the children). The effect was very pretty.'[54]

The Archbishop was very gracious and spoke kindly to Mary regretting that he had to leave early and could not give out all the prizes. Mary wanted to be at all these displays and prize-givings even though it entailed a mighty effort on her part. She took pride in what the sisters were accomplishing and saw it as her duty to support them, not to mention her own pride in the achievements of the children.

That Christmas Day was a peaceful one for Mary even though she had to travel from the North Shore to the Providence for dinner but this, too, was a pleasant experience and she noted in her diary that she had a happy, peaceful day.

---

52. Mary MacKillop's Diary, 20 December 1884.
53. Mary MacKillop's Diary, 1 January 1885.
54. Mary MacKillop's Diary, 22 December 1884.

Chapter Four
1885, A Memorable Year

After a retreat which commenced on Sunday 28 December, four sisters received the habit at the hands of the Archbishop. The ceremony took place at St Michael's Church next to the Providence. The Novitiate in Sydney was up and running but the small chapel at North Sydney was unsuitable for Reception and Profession ceremonies. St Michael's Church was owned by the Marist Fathers.

Concern for the spiritual needs of the sisters in country places prompted Mary to write to Archbishop Moran regarding this deprivation:

> There are only two places in the Archdiocese where the Sisters have to fast for the late Mass on Sundays, and where they have no opportunity of receiving Holy Communion on week mornings instead. Bulli and Jamberoo are the places I mean. The Sisters have a comfortable convent at Bulli, and the great privilege of the Most Holy Sacrament in their oratory. But up to the present, their pastor has not seen his way to arrange for them to receive Holy Communion but at a late Mass on Sundays. The Sisters at Jamberoo occupy a small rented cottage and have no suitable room for an Oratory. Their privation is greater, but has been cheerfully accepted in the full hope that as soon as possible it would be made lighter, and so I am sure it will.
>
> I don't think Father Riorden liked to undertake anything in the way of building there until Your Grace would arrive and see for yourself. I may mention that the convent furniture at Jamberoo has not yet been paid for, but I do not think that the

> Committee will neglect it any longer; perhaps they have paid for it since Xmas. I would not trouble Your Grace with these matters just now but that you kindly told me to do so, and I humbly submit that I in no way wish to blame any pastor.
>
> The Sisters at Dapto and Albion Park are comfortably situated and Father Ryan is very attentive to their spiritual wants. The Dapto School is a small one and the people might pay much better than they do, but the Sisters manage to keep out of debt and are very happy. There is no Extraordinary for any of the convents out of Sydney, therefore, if Your Grace will, at your convenience, kindly appoint any you please, we shall be very grateful. Father Muraire S.M. is the Extraordinary for the Providence, and Your Grace named him for the Novitiate, for which I am very thankful, but I have not been able to see him to mention the matter.[1]

It must be remembered that at this time, fasting for Holy Communion required Catholics to abstain, even from a drink of water, from midnight until after Mass. Besides this, Mass could not be celebrated after midday. This was a difficult requirement both for priest and people given the harsh summer climate in Australia and the need for late Masses on a Sunday morning in country parishes.

The Archbishop wished the sisters to open a school at Bankstown (called Irishtown because of the large number of Irish people in the area). Mary was able to write and tell him that

> Sister Bernard and I went out to Bankstown yesterday and think the situation for a school and orphanage a most delightful one. We were told by one of the State school teachers that there are 40 Catholic children attending the school there. I wish we had Sisters to send there at once, but even if we had, there is no house yet.[2]

---

1. Mary MacKillop to Archbishop Moran, 20 January 1885. The 'Extraordinary' was the name given to a priest who was appointed by the Archbishop to hear the confessions of the sisters in a particular convent. He visited the convent four times a year. This term distinguished him from the 'Ordinary Confessor who was usually resident in the place where the convent was situated and heard the sisters' confessions each week.
2. Mary MacKillop to Archbishop Moran, 22 January 1885.

To her mother she wrote in March:

> Yesterday our five novices were professed at St Michael's.[3] The church was crowded. Many fashionable friends were there—amongst them Sir Patrick Jennings and Lady Jennings, Mrs Young, etc. etc., the Archbishop, Vicar General, and many priests. The ceremonies went off splendidly—not one hitch or mistake being made. St Michael's choir, aided by some friendly professionals attended and sang beautifully. His Grace preached a long sermon upon St Joseph and spoke most feelingly and affectionately to the sisters. I had a great deal to do during the Retreat.[4]

Mary certainly would have spent many hours preparing the novices for the ceremonies and nothing less than perfection would have satisfied her—she wanted the outward to reflect the inner joy of the young women.

The number of novices had grown and Dean Kenny was worried that they would run out of room so he was trying to buy a house and ground adjoining Dr Clarke's which would give them room to build a chapel.

Later on that year she wrote to her mother that Uncle Donald's daughter, eighteen-year-old Maggie

> has improved wonderfully in every way. As we cannot get a suitable Music Teacher for Moss Vale, she is going there for three months and so will earn something and have ample time to practise and be better able to profit by a master's lessons afterwards. She has decided talent of every kind.[5]

Mary was very interested in these cousins and, as they were excellent musicians, often called upon them to take up the role of music teacher when, as has already been mentioned, schools required one.

---

3. The five novices were Sisters Evangelista Carr, Isabelle Colvin, Cecilia Quilty, Norbert Quilty and Blandina O'Donnell.
4. Mary MacKillop to Flora, 20 March 1885.
5. Mary MacKillop to Flora, 1 July 1885.

To Cardinal Simeoni in July, she wrote:

> The sufferings—I may say persecutions—of our Sisters in Adelaide have become so great that I am reluctantly compelled to appeal to Your Eminence's fatherly protection against the acts of the Bishop in their regard. As long as I alone was made to feel the consequences of His Lordship's displeasure, and that I had no serious fears of his interfering too much with our Constitutions, I thought it my duty to submit quietly and wait until it would please God to bring about peace with the Bishop again.[6]

The situation of the sisters in Adelaide was causing Mary great distress and worry and her inability to be there in person exacerbated this. She had to be careful to whom and what she wrote as tales were carried to Bishop Reynolds who was trying to force the Adelaide sisters to break with Mary and put themselves under his authority alone. Matters were not helped by the appointment of Father Polk sj who had succeeded Father Tappeiner as the sisters' confessor. He was known to carry tales about the sisters to the Bishop and this created further mischief and did not help the sisters' cause.

During Easter week 1885 the situation in Adelaide reached a major climax with Bishop Reynolds declaring to the sisters that he alone was their Superior, that he had received letters from Rome during Passion Week declaring that the congregation was to be divided into diocesan communities and the Bishop in each case to be the Superior in his own diocese. He declared that Mother Mary's authority had ceased and he ordered each sister to make her decision as to whether she would accept his authority or not. The sisters asked for time to consider but all were resolved to keep to the constitutions and central government.[7]

Sister Evelyn Pickering could write in 1983 that:

> One of the outstanding revelations concerning the Easter week campaign against the Sisters was the extent to which the Bishop and his Vicar General could go to force the

---

6. Mary MacKillop to Cardinal Simeoni, July 1885.
7. Marie Therese Foale, *Never See a Need: The Sisters of St Joseph in South Australia 1866–2010* (Trustees of the Sisters of St Joseph, 2016), 124.

> Sisters into an acceptance of their plans. At first there were threats—<u>Sydney would not receive them</u>. But Sydney would! Threats gave way to prohibition to be carried out by virtue of obedience —<u>No passage money was to be provided</u>.[8]

Mary encouraged the sisters to remain with their schools but many of them were at breaking point and longed to get away from Adelaide. She was able to organise for the steamship company to give passages for those who wanted to go to Sydney. Sister Monica quietly sent the novices to Sydney in May and other sisters soon followed.

In a letter to Sister Monica, Mary urged her to advise the sisters to keep on the schools

> if they can. Advise them to suffer anything short of consenting to separation rather than have to leave the place without Sisters. Of course, those who are really in danger or whom the Bishop particularly dislikes had better leave as quietly as they can. If they would only have courage and not be afraid of his threat of expulsion, I would tell them wait on. Rome will not force anything upon them.[9]

Marie Therese Foale rsj commented:

> For some it was too difficult and they went to Sydney. For his part Moran appears to have been pleased that so many Sisters were coming into his diocese for he was in desperate need of Religious to manage his Catholic schools and this was an opportunity for him to obtain the services of a significant number of experienced teachers, without effort or cost to himself or the diocese.[10]

When Mary wrote to Sister Raymond in New Zealand she told her that all of the professed sisters who had come from South Australia were more or less ill and not able for any duty immediately. In a PS to this letter she wrote:

---

8. *Resource Material from the Archives of the Sisters of St Joseph of the Sacred Heart*. Issue No. 9, January 1983, 76.
9. Mary MacKillop to Sister Monica Phillips, 21 April 1885.
10. Foale, *Never See a Need*, 124.

> Sisters Gertrude [Hayman], Ambrosine [O'Donnell], Agatha [Nolan], Eugenius [Raftery], F. Xavier [Amsinck], M Josephine [Mahony] and Agnes [Smith], six novices and two postulants have come over. Only three of the Professed are well.[11]

In all, over fifty sisters made the move to New South Wales causing schools to be closed in South Australia.[12]

When Mary received a reply to her July 1884 letter to Cardinal Simeoni she could pass on the news to Sister Monica that

> the Bishop has <u>no authority</u> for what he has done. He is sure to be censured. The Irish Bishops will do their utmost at the Synod to have our Institute made Diocesan, but will fail if the Sisters hold out as they have done and are doing. Rome is very jealous of its authority, and the manner in which it has been set aside in Adelaide will not help the Bishop's cause.[13]

How right Mary was about Rome's regard for its authority as future events were to prove.

Meanwhile in New South Wales the foundations went on as the *Catholic Directory* of 1885

> gives two foundations of the Sisters at Granville and Rookwood (Lidcombe). A convent at Granville was provided first for the community serving the parochial school there, and from there two Sisters went to Lidcombe to teach the children in the home of Edmund and Johanna Keating until a school was provided.[14]

Rookwood (Lidcombe) became a parish in May 1885 and Father Furlong was appointed the parish priest. His parish included Irish Town and St Anne's, Concord. The corner stone of the church/school was blessed on 4 April 1886.[15] When completed the sisters were able to conduct school in this building.

---

11. Mary MacKillop to Sister Raymond Smyth, 6 May 1885.
12. Thirteen schools closed in South Australia during this period.
13. Mary MacKillop to Sister Monica Phillips, 21 April 1885.
14. Burford, *Unfurrowed Fields*, 59.
15. *Freeman's Journal*, 10 April 1886, 15.

St Joseph's Convent Lidcombe NSW. Undated.

In a letter to her mother dated 1 July 1885, Mary wrote

> Archdeacon Rigney has obtained his foundation for Granville and is one of our kindest priests and friends. Our dear little Sister Gertrude (Hayman) is at Granville. She has lost her mother who died since she left Adelaide and you may be sure is grieved. Please send her a few lines. She will value it so much from you. Poor little Sister M. Christopher is also in great sorrow. She has lost a dear mother, a saintly woman, who died from internal cancer. She would treasure a few lines from Grandma. [16]

St Joseph's Convent Granville NSW. c.1906.

---

16. Mary MacKillop to Flora, 1 July 1885.

Sister Gertrude had accompanied the novices to Sydney when they left South Australia in late April.¹⁷ One of them was Sister Ann Joseph Waters who, after her profession in May 1885, spent some time at Granville before being transferred to Kincumber where she laboured for the remainder of her religious life. Flora knew many of the sisters and 'Grandma' was the title that they gave her.

Flora MacKillop.

Another piece of news in this July letter referred to the novices:

> We have 23 novices here now – none in Adelaide. Postulants come from all parts. Two Bathurst Sisters have returned to us.

Who were these two Bathurst sisters and why did they return to the North Sydney Josephites? The answer regarding one sister lies in the obituary for a Perthville sister, Regis Forde. When Regis joined the Perthville sisters two of her sisters, Sisters Anne and Alphonsus had been there for three years. All three women had come under the influence of Father Julian Tenison Woods in Sydney and had been directed by him to the diocesan foundation at Perthville. The obituary noted that

---

17. The novices were Sisters Ann Joseph Waters, James Feehan, Clare O'Donnell, Finbar Foley, Walburgh Bannock and Imelda Gleeson. The postulants were Sisters Columba O'Brien, Romaeus Sheehan and Sylvester Higgins.

> Sister Regis' two blood sisters transferred to the Sisters of
> St Joseph at North Sydney: in 1885 Sister Anne and in 1887
> Sister Alphonsus. The former ministered for many years
> in New Zealand where she is buried. The latter was in the
> Wilcannia diocese when it was separated from the Bathurst
> Diocese and she transferred along with other Josephite Sisters
> from the Diocese, to North Sydney.[18]

The date of Sister Alphonsus' transfer was not 1887 but 1902. Sister Anne was sent almost immediately to the South Island of New Zealand, probably to Temuka, where as a music teacher she was most welcome. She taught music very successfully in South Canterbury and later on prepared sisters for music examinations. The name of the other sister who transferred from Bathurst in 1885 remains a mystery. So, too, do the reasons for their transfer.

Again the *Catholic Directory* had an entry that stated that the Catholic school at Menangle in the Campbelltown district was in the care of the sisters from 1885.[19]

The following information concerning the history of Menangle appeared in *The Voice of the North*:

> When State aid to denominational schools ceased the Sisters
> of St Joseph took charge of the school at Menangle and
> conducted it for some years, but were eventually obliged to
> close it by reason of the dwindling of the population which
> followed the extension of the railway system south, west and
> north ... the old church and school is now only a memory
> with the few remaining who were educated within its walls on
> weekdays, and who worshipped in it on Sundays.[20]

The sisters left Menangle in 1893, thirty-five years before the above was written. They withdrew when the new railway line by-passed the town and there was a consequent decline in the school enrolment.

Mary wrote to Sister Raymond Smyth expressing her difficulties in regard to finding sisters for various places telling her: 'we are even now in a fix for sisters for the different places. We must send one

---

18. Archives of the Sisters of St Joseph. Obituary, 8 December 1938.
19. Burford, *Unfurrowed Fields*, 61.
20. *The Voice of the North*, 12 November 1928, 14.

foundation to Narrabri in Armidale (this has been promised for three years)'.[21]

To her mother she wrote in July about the foundation at Narrabri:

> We are to make a new foundation in Armidale diocese this week. A beautiful convent is being built, and until it is ready, the Pastor—a most holy man—has given up his presbytery as a temporary convent and gone himself into lodgings.[22]

The holy pastor of Narrabri, Father J Doyle soon reported to Mother Mary that the sisters 'are getting on well with the children . . . the people are delighted . . . we all feel ourselves under a deep obligation of gratitude to you and your Order.'[23]

Thus the foundation of Narrabri began but, as we shall see, it was only to be for a few years until 'by negotiations through Bishop Torreggiani and the Sisters of St Joseph, the Sisters of Mercy took up the work of Catholic education in Narrabri in 1889'.[24]

The Sisters of Mercy had become established at Grafton and were able to make new foundations so they were able to move to Narrabri in 1889 and Inverell in 1891, leaving the sisters available for other foundations in the Armidale Diocese. Both Narrabri and Inverell were large towns. The Josephites left for the smaller, more isolated ones.

That September of 1885 brought great joy and gladness to Mary with the news of her brother Donald's ordination as a Jesuit priest in Wales on 20 September. In the letter with the announcement, Donald told Mary that 'you have your long-cherished wish. I am a priest of the Society of Jesus. What a fine cry you will have over this!'[25] He included, on separate pieces of paper, his first written blessing to Mary and another to his family. Mary's heart sang praises and thanks to God for the happiness that this news brought to her and to her mother, Flora, and her sister, Annie. Now they and all their family could look forward to the return of Father Donald MacKillop.

---

21. Mary MacKillop to Sister Raymond Smyth, 30 June 1885.
22. Mary MacKillop to Flora, 1 July 1885.
23. Father J Doyle to Mary MacKillop, 13 August 1885.
24. Burford, *Unfurrowed Fields*, 64.
25. Donald MacKillop to Mary MacKillop, 20 September 1885.

Father Donald MacKillop.

Mary took a short break in Queensland before October 1885. In a letter to Mary, Sister Borgia Fay said that she hoped that, as she put it, Mary's 'short trip to Queensland has improved your health which needs strengthening to bear the long strain of anxiety and suspense you have undergone.'[26]

But another upheaval was about to descend upon the sisters with the return of Cardinal Moran from Rome. This took place towards the end of 1885 for with the Cardinal came news for the Sisters of St Joseph. Mary wrote to Sister Monica:

> At last we have news from Rome and thank God we are protected there. The Constitutions are upheld, Mother House also, but my last election is declared invalid on the plea of an interval having been necessary before a fresh election such as was made. The Cardinal was deputed to make this known to me, and to appoint a temporary Sup. Genl. until there could be a fresh election at a General Chapter.[27]

How much Cardinal Moran had to do with this appointment is a matter of conjecture but with the situation in Adelaide no closer to solution, apparently, he might have deemed it wiser to replace Mary

---

26. Sister Borgia Fay to Mary MacKillop, 22 October 1885.
27. Mary MacKillop to Sister Monica Phillips, 12 November 1885.

with a more pliant Mother General. From a list of names given by Mary and her Councillors, the Cardinal chose Sister Bernard Walsh and appointed her to succeed Mother Mary who, with characteristic humility, accepted this appointment. All thought it would be just a temporary one, but it was to last more than twelve years and the Cardinal was prepared to extend it for a further five years had not death intervened. These twelve years were to prove difficult ones for Mary as Mother Bernard, whilst being an efficient Provincial with the support of Mary, was not a match for the dynamic and decisive Mary. However, she was popular with the many Irish Bishops and clerics and could appease them in a way that Mary could not.

His Eminence Patrick Francis Cardinal Moran. Mother Bernard Walsh.

At this time, Mary was very concerned about the forthcoming Synod of Bishops which was to take place in November 1885. She realised that they would discuss the matter of the Sisters of St Joseph of the Sacred Heart and their Central Government. Both Bishops Matthew and James Quinn were dead by this time but there were other bishops who wanted the sisters to be diocesan. Letters went from Mother Bernard and from the sisters in South Australia to Cardinal Simeoni in Rome asking that the Central Government be upheld. Mother Bernard was urged to write at Mary's instigation and probably Mary actually dictated the letter since she knew the authorities personally.

As Paul Gardiner sj put it in his book, *Mary MacKillop, An Extraordinary Australian*:

> When the decrees of the Synod became known, it was clear that the concern of the sisters had been justified. The bishops had voted that they should be a diocesan institute. Decree 99 read: With regard to the Congregation which is called Sisters of St Joseph of the Sacred Heart, the Bishops think fit that the convents or Religious Houses in each Diocese should be subject to their respective Ordinaries, like the Sisters of Mercy.[28]

Fortunately for the sisters, the Congregation of Propaganda struck out this Decree, but this was not known until 1888.

During the time of the Synod, Mary and the sisters had visits from friends among the clergy and one surprise:

> Reynolds actually came to see the Josephites, and spoke as if nothing had broken their friendship. Not only that, but Russell turned up too.[29] Mary was convinced that Moran had put the pressure of Christian charity on both.[30]

The visit of Bishop Reynolds pleased Mary since he had not come near her when he was in Sydney in 1884.

Archbishop Christopher Augustine Reynolds.

---

28. Gardiner, *Mary MacKillop*, 343.
29. Archdeacon Russell was the Vicar General at the time when Mary was expelled from Adelaide.
30. Gardiner, Mary MacKillop, 343.

The flow of vocations to the Novitiate in North Sydney was a constant source of encouragement and gratitude for Mary and those early sisters were privileged to have the Foundress as their Mistress of Novices. About this time there were twenty-one novices and five more were about to be admitted to the novitiate.

Chapter Five
Joys and Sorrows of 1886

An early example of Mary's acceptance of her new role is revealed in a letter to her mother on 22 March 1886 from Mount Street, North Sydney reminding her:

> You know I have been going to school since Christmas. Now Mother Bernard wants me to take sole charge of the Bazaar business, so I must leave the school for the greater part of the week to Sister Mary Gertrude and her assistants.[1]

Mary was in her element teaching and assisting the poor children at St John's Poor School, Kent Street. In that same letter we learn that Mary had been asked by Mother Bernard to go to Moss Vale where Father Petre, her old friend of Dapto and Albion Park days, was now parish priest. Some trouble had erupted between the priest and parishioners and involved the sisters, so Mary's negotiating skills were needed to defuse that situation. This she did to the satisfaction of all. How many other such situations was she called on to settle?

From June 1885 Mary had been negotiating with the parish priest of Araluen regarding the building of a convent for a proposed foundation. She had written to Father Mahoney on 30 June 1885 as follows:

> I received your letter on Saturday, too late to reply by that day's post. As I see that you are also anxious that we should take the school, and as the responsibility of building is not to rest upon us, we hope to have Sisters ready for it by the New Year.

---

1. Mary MacKillop to Flora, 22 March 1886.

> Will you kindly tell the Committee that we require at least six rooms, and as they have so little money, we think it would be better if you and they should decide as to which kind of building would be the cheapest.[2]

Mary, herself, wrote to Committee member, Mr O'Reilly, in reply to his letter:

> I have written to Father Mahoney and mentioned the number of rooms we should have for any comfort and which I hope you will see your way to provide. Knowing how limited your means are, I do not like to propose any decided plan.
>
> I don't think you can possibly build under £300, but should imagine that if you have £200, the other one hundred as well as what you will require for furnishing can be obtained, say, at the opening, or by children's concerts, or such means.[3]

Mary had learned how unwise it was to send sisters to these distant places without stipulating that a decent place was to be provided for them to live in and that it was necessary for the place to be ready for them or at least be in the building process.

In 1886 the foundation was made in that gold mining town of Araluen 'an extensive valley surrounded by precipitous mountains of the coast range over 3000 feet high'.[4]

From another source we learn:

> When the sisters came to open a school at Araluen in 1886 they stayed for nine months at the Perseverance Hotel before their convent was ready. The strict religious discipline of the Catholic home was carried over into the management of the hotel. No drunkenness was allowed; swearing was forbidden as was card-playing and any type of gambling. Men were not served unless they were supporting their wives sufficiently, and cheques could not be cashed unless the wife gave her consent.[5]

---

2. Mary MacKillop to Fr Mahoney, 30 June 1885.
3. Mary MacKillop to Mr O'Reilly, 30 June 1885.
4. *Freeman's Journal*, 30 September 1909, 57.
5. Sisters of St Joseph NSW Province, *Our Foundation Story Issue 4*, 31 August 2003.

This was surely a suitable temporary place for the sisters to occupy until the convent was completed.

Araluan church, school and convent Araluen NSW. Undated. Photo provided by Clem Wilson, Araluen. Used with permission.

When the Auxiliary Bishop of Sydney, the Right Rev Dr Higgins, paid an Episcopal visitation to Araluen on Monday 11 November 1889, he

> formally blessed and opened the convent, after which a display was given by the school children, under the direction of the good Sisters of St Joseph, who have been so untiring and energetic ever since their arrival. The plain and fancy work was much praised and admired by the Bishop, as also was the vocal and declamatory performances of the children.[6]

The convent had been occupied well before this date so the 'opening' was merely a formality.

In an article in *The Catholic Press* entitled 'Here and There', Araluen is said to have had, at one time, a population of 34,000 people who lived and prospered from the gold found in the sandy bed of the Araluen Creek. The author went on to say:

---

6. *Freeman's Journal*, 23 November 1889, 16.

> The Catholic schools, convent and presbytery betray no indication of past prosperity. They are modest, plain bundles of sticks, and I marvel much that not one nugget of the gold that was at one time so common seems to have been devoted to the cause of religion or education.
>
> The little Catholic school is under the direction of the self-denying Sisters of St. Joseph. The Sisters seem to live for the children of the district, and it is marvellous how they live at all. Their school is well taught.[7]

St Joseph's School Araluen NSW.

As we have seen, the foundations that followed in the year 1886 had already been negotiated by Mary. Another foundation was made at the request of the Bishop of Armidale who held her in high regard and was a true supporter of her and the sisters. So Uralla in the Armidale Diocese opened on 1 January 1886. In preparation for the coming of the sisters, Bishop Torreggiani had blessed and laid the foundation stone for the convent on 18 October 1885. This was reported in the *Freeman's Journal* which also gave this information:

> It may be of interest to readers to learn that the weatherboard schoolroom is being erected with the materials of which the old chapel was built, and which has been taken down and removed to the convent site. Though put up about 28 years ago, the timber has been found equal to new, and it is calculated that, through the material being retained instead of sold for the sum offered for it (£15), a saving of £200 has been effected.[8]

---

7. *The Catholic Press*, 24 April 1897, 18.
8. *Freeman's Journal*, 31 October 1885, 9.

So all was prepared for the arrival of the sisters with convent and schoolroom ready to receive them. The four sisters lost no time setting up the school and, as in so many instances, putting on concerts and organising bazaars.

Another article from the *Freeman's Journal* in the September after their arrival told of their musical ability:

> The good Sisters of St. Joseph, who have worked with marked success since their arrival amongst us, have a very nice school with an average attendance of about 55 children ... In addition to their work in the school, the Sisters, with a number of their pupils, have undertaken the singing in the church. The sweet, fresh voices of the children, strengthened by the musical and splendid voices of their teachers, form a very nice choir, which will ere long compare very favourably with any choir in New England.[9]

In October 1888, the sisters advertised the convent as a Boarding School for young ladies in the *Freeman's Journal*. The cost was £32 per annum. A comprehensive curriculum included 'Piano and Vocal Music, Drawing, Plain and Fancy Needlework of all Descriptions, Wax Flowers, Painting, Bead and Leather Work'.[10]

St Joseph's Convent Uralla NSW. c.1906.

---

9. *Freeman's Journal*, 25 September 1886, 10.
10. *Freeman's Journal*, 27 October 1888, 11.

Such were the beginnings of the work of the Josephites in the town of Uralla.

In its issue of 23 January 1886 the *Freeman's Journal* announced that St Fiacre's Church/School at Leichhardt would be opened on 31 January 1886. The foundation stone was blessed and laid on 19 April 1885. It also announced that

> a mixed school will be opened in the above mentioned church building by the Sisters of Saint Joseph from Camperdown on Monday 18th inst.[11]

Initially they lived at Annandale and it was said that the residents could set their watches as the sisters walked from there to St Fiacre's School. When St Martha's Leichhardt opened they walked daily from there until the people found a convent for them. It seemed that in those pioneer days it was necessary to be good at walking because they did so much of it.

Whilst these foundations were being made in 1886, as has already been noted, Mother Bernard asked Mary to take charge of the organisation of the great bazaar which she did with all her usual efficiency, persuading many prominent women to take stalls. This bazaar was a grand affair according to the report in the *Sydney Morning Herald* and showed the extent of the organisation on the part of Mary who appealed to many of the leading women of Sydney at the time to take up stalls. She called upon the sisters to support the eight stalls: Scottish, French, Spanish, Irish, Australian, St Joseph's Children's, Convent and Refreshment as the report indicated. It was held in the Masonic Hall in the city and was in aid of the St Joseph's Providence.[12]

Such an undertaking called for all Mary's time and people skills to persuade these ladies to be responsible for stalls as well as canvassing stores and her many friends to donate saleable goods. She wanted to ensure the best financial result possible for the upkeep of the poor at the Providence.

It was during this Bazaar that Mary received the tragic news of the wreck of the *Ly-ee-Moon* off Green Cape and the drowning of her mother, Flora. Flora was on her way from Melbourne to help with the Bazaar and was carrying with her many articles she had collected for

---

11. *Freeman's Journal*, 23 January 1886, 11.
12. *The Sydney Morning Herald*, 1 June 1886, 4.

the stalls in Melbourne as well as a lot of her own needlework. Mary wrote to her sister, Annie:

> God help us all. The hand of God is heavy upon us, but His holy Will must be done. Oh, Annie, I had so yearned to see her again, and all the Sisters were planning to make her visit a bright and happy one. Poor, dear, long-suffering Mamma. I am sure she has gone to a well-deserved rest and will no longer have to feel her dependent position.[13]

Mary's sorrow was intense but some relief came when she received news that her mother's body was rescued from the sea, intact. She acquired lead for the coffin and her cousin, John McDonald, who was at home with his parents at the time, travelled to Eden to identify the body, have the lead coffin made up and escort the precious remains to Sydney. The Requiem Mass was celebrated at St Michael's Church in the Providence grounds and the burial took place in the little cemetery in the grounds at St Charles' Church, Ryde.[14]

Mary's health was a problem during this time after her mother's death but she kept going although she was ill for more than a month during July and August. She was only able to write to Sister Raymond Smyth in late August about the Profession ceremony when

> the Cardinal himself professed 11 Sisters on the 2nd July— amongst these Sisters Bernadette and Clare, two of the best Sisters we have got, also Sister Dorothea. Sister Clare went almost immediately to Glen Innes.[15]

Mary wrote further about a situation regarding Adelaide that had caused her much anxiety and was the cause of her illness. She told Sister Raymond that

---

13. Mary MacKillop to Annie MacKillop, 1 June 1886.
14. Flora's remains were exhumed from this cemetery and transferred to the Sisters' part of Macquarie Park Cemetery in 1973 when it was proposed to make the little cemetery at St Charles' Church Ryde into a car park. This proposal did not eventuate and the cemetery remains.
15. Mary MacKillop to Sister Raymond Smyth, 2 July 1886. Those professed were Sisters Bernadette Goodwin (Temuka NZ), Clare Fitzpatrick and Dorothea O'Neill.

> I am dreadfully pained about some Adelaide business. Only fancy, they have been wanting me to sign a paper making myself <u>personally responsible</u> for £2,000, the old mortgage on the Kensington property. I cannot go into details but, if I did this, I would be as good as making a present of that amount to Dr Reynolds for he has some hold on the place. The manner in which I have been deceived in this is like all the rest—and not I alone but my good faithful Sisters with me. It may be that I shall have to go over to Adelaide before the affair can be settled. All this business has pained and upset me more that I can express.[16]

Bishop Reynolds was certainly not Mary's friend and appeared to be taking every opportunity to persecute and humiliate her as well as her faithful sisters in Adelaide who were struggling to pay interest on the mortgages on the Kensington property and also other properties that Mary had bought in places where the people were too poor to provide the sisters with suitable accommodation.

The conclusion to this letter contains an interesting line where she asks that 'God bless all my <u>dear faithful children</u>. As MF I may say this but not as <u>MG</u>'.[17] (She could say this as Mother Foundress but not as Mother General).[18] This is one of the few times that Mary claimed her title of Foundress although she was always regarded as such by the sisters.

Mossman school was opened by the Sisters of Mercy who withdrew from there in June 1886. The school was handed over to the Josephites soon afterwards and four of them caught the tram each day from Mount Street to Ridge Street North Sydney and then walked through the park to Military Road.[19] Mary noted in her diary the many times she visited this school. She also noted the school fees that were collected and handed to her and were a great help in providing for the novices and postulants and the sisters who cared for them.

Mother Bernard relied on Mary's help in carrying out her duties as Mother General and it was often Mary's task to write letters for her as this one to Sister Raymond Smyth shows:

---

16. Mary MacKillop to Sister Raymond Smyth, 2 July 1886.
17. Mary MacKillop to Sister Raymond Smyth, 2 July 1886.
18. MG was the abbreviation for Mother General, the title given to the leader of the Institute.
19. Mossman later called Mosman.

The Sisters must tell you all the news. I only came in from Rookwood and had given up any idea of writing to you today, but as M.G. cannot get a moment, she has asked me to do so for her.[20]

Mary's life was a busy one as so much work fell to her and the constant mental as well as physical strain often saw her having days of ill health. So that difficult year of 1886 passed away.

---

20. Mary MacKillop to Sister Raymond Smyth, 20 August 1886.

Chapter Six
New Beginnings in 1887

To her good friend Sister Andrea Howley, Mary opened her heart in the new year of 1887:

> What a sad Xmas you all had. Poor Sister Joseph's was a fearful—but I hope for her a happy death. I hold her, the poor child, blameless, but what can I say of those who put so great a strain as that oath upon her poor weak mind, who came between her and her duty to her Superiors? Let us say God forgive them. Poor Sister Francis de Sales [Sullivan] had her eyes opened a little before the end came, and died in peace. The news of Sister Joseph's death, even before I heard any of the particulars, gave me a great shock and made me cry more bitterly than the death of any Sister had ever done. Then, when the sad truth came, I cannot describe what I felt. For a while it was hard to feel that I could forgive. The wonder is that more victims have not gone, but somehow I don't think any of us will have the same heart and nerve as before that dreadful time. I know I never will.[1]

Such were the effects of that so-called Apostolic Commission of 1883 and the oath of secrecy imposed on the sisters. Sister Joseph Lonergan suffered a nervous breakdown as a result of the strain that the oath, forced upon her at the time of the Commission, had upon her mind. Sadly she was committed to the Adelaide Asylum and died there at the end of December 1886. Mary did not allow bitterness to creep into her thoughts of those responsible and forgive she did, but at what cost? The oath that the sisters were forced to take, had it

---

1. Mary MacKillop to Sister Andrea Howley, 26 January 1887.

been publicly known, could have had serious civil repercussions for Bishop Reynolds and Archdeacon Russell as it was against civil law. What lengths these two men went to, especially Archdeacon Russell, to heap ignominy on Mary and her sisters. It was fortunate for them that Mary counselled her sisters to bear all in silence.

Mary wrote to Sister Andrea about the Retreat and her part in it, her subsequent illness and then about the business she was conducting with regard to the two terrace houses facing Mount Street. The Dean had left his house to be used for aged priests but eventually the Cardinal allowed it to be rented to the sisters for a nominal rent. The adjoining house the sisters purchased for £1,000 cash. She organised for the folding doors in two front rooms of what was the Dean's house to be taken down and then this large room was used as a lovely Oratory. It was the worry of this business that brought on a severe illness for Mary.

In a footnote to this letter Mary wrote of the illness of Terry Woods.[2] Father Woods had come from Queensland to visit him but did not come near Mary or the sisters. This caused deep sorrow to her but she visited Terry when she could.[3]

After his scientific expedition to Malaya and work in the Northern Territory, Father Woods settled with some ex–sisters in Sydney about June 1887. Mary had always sent greetings to him on his birthday, 15 November. She did this in 1887 and received a polite reply but he declined to renew contact with her or her sisters or receive any visits from them. When Sister Monica wrote to him on the death of his brother, Terry, he replied saying in part that

> Mother Mary was kind enough to ask permission to come and see me, but I was obliged to decline. Under no circumstances could I consent to renew my relations with your Institute.[4]

Mary persisted and eventually he acceded to her request to visit and wrote: 'Well, my dear Mother Mary, if you insist upon this, I must defer to your wishes' and added in a postscript 'If you will write and say when you will call, I will take care to be at home for you. Between 3 and 5 in the afternoon is the best time.'[5] Mary did visit him although she was not well received by the other residents of the house. There does not seem to be

---

2. Terry Woods was one of Father Julian Woods' brothers.
3. Mary MacKillop to Sister Andrea Howley, 26 January 1887.
4. Father Woods to Sister Monica, 15 July 1887.
5. Father Woods to Mary MacKillop, 12 August 1887.

an account of what passed between them on these visits. She had heard that he liked strawberries and she tried now and then to send him some.[6]

Father Julian Tenison Woods. 1875.

The sisters were concerned that the Sacred Congregation in Rome would favour the Bishops' desire for the Institute to be made Diocesan and, at the express wish of Mother Bernard, Mary wrote to Dr Campbell again pleading for Central Government to be upheld. She made another request that

> our great hope is that the Mother House will be transferred to Sydney, and that we may soon have our General Chapter here. It would surely never do to have it under the Presidency of the Archbishop of Adelaide who has proved himself the Institute's most bitter enemy.[7]

In 1887 Cardinal Moran, who was not at all happy with the idea of having elderly women and young boys living together at the Providence, put the presbytery and church grounds at Kincumber at the disposal of the sisters. This he did formally on 19 March 1887. Two sisters were appointed to live in this cottage and prepare for the future

---

6. Mary MacKillop to Sisters Monica and Mechtilde, 10 October 1889.
7. Mary MacKillop to Dr Campbell, Scots College Rome, 20 September 1887.

of the orphanage. They were accompanied by two boys from the Providence and from April 1887 until the end of 1888, the numbers grew gradually until there were three sisters and twenty-two boys living at Kincumber.

Sister Philippa O'Callaghan, a sister who had spent her entire religious life caring for the orphans in Adelaide, was sent to Kincumber in 1887. She oversaw the extension of the accommodation at the cottage by building an oratory and two visitors' rooms with verandah attached. At right angles to these were added two large dormitories and a boys' refectory as well as the kitchen. Over the coming years the number of sisters increased from three to six and then eventually there were ten sisters and sixty orphan boys.

Mary took a great interest in the orphanage and visited there as often as she could. Her love encompassed those little boys who loved her in return. Sister Philippa moved to Victoria in the mid-1890s when she was replaced by Sister Ann Joseph Waters who had moved to Kincumber soon after her profession and spent the remainder of her life there. She lies buried in the little cemetery near the church.

St Joseph's Convent Kincumber South NSW.

Meanwhile other country foundations were going ahead. In June 1887, Cardinal Moran advised the parish priest of Bombala that the Sisters of St Joseph would take over the convent and school about to be relinquished by the Sisters of Charity who had come to Bombala in January 1885 and established a Primary and a High school. The sisters were asked to arrive at the end of June when the Sisters of Charity were leaving and were told to be ready to begin school on the following Monday. At the end of the year 1887 they arranged a concert that was reported in *The Freeman's Journal*:

> There could not have been less than from 250 to 300 persons present in the room. The children under the Sisters' instructions gave an entertainment to their parents and friends which could not be surpassed in Sydney. A few months ago three Sisters of St Joseph came to Bombala, took charge of the convent and school, and since then by their kindness, Christianity and charity have won the love of the children attending the school, and the esteem of Catholics and all others in the district. The schoolroom was beautifully decorated and the children, over 100 in number, were all tastefully dressed. The girls were in white some of them wearing green and blue and pink scarfs. More than thanks is due from the parents of the children to Miss Vider, the music teacher, for the efficient way in which the pupils performed the musical pieces.[8]

It had taken the sisters only a short time to arrange the concert, probably aimed at showing the people what they could do and also to help pay off any debts they owed. Before their coming the convent and school had been in an old hotel and so priest and people soon planned to build a new convent.

Convent Bombala, NSW. 1993.

---

8. *Freeman's Journal*, 31 December 1887, 9.

Around the same time there was another movement among the sisters when it was decided to close the school at Jamberoo. In July, Sisters Eulalia McDermott and Magdalen Thompson moved from Jamberoo to Kiama where the railway had just arrived, bypassing Jamberoo. At first the sisters lived in a house owned by the Ettinghausen family and taught school in the Church. Later the parish priest, Father McDonnell, purchased from the Railways Department a building which had been used as a school for the children of the railway men when the line was extended from Kiama to Nowra. This building served as a school for many long years.

Convent Kiama, NSW. 1993.

Catholic Church Kiama. NSW. Photo courtesy of Kiama Municipal Council Photographic Collection.

Bishop Higgins performed the blessing of the foundation stone of the new convent, a brick building adjacent to St Peter's Church, on 15 September 1889. The children of St Joseph's School presented the Bishop with a silver inkstand.[9] Cardinal Moran blessed and opened the new convent on 16 February 1890.[10]

Mary and Sister Bernard had visited the site for a school at Bankstown in January 1885 and had declared it to be very suitable for the purpose. However, it was not opened until 1887. At first the sisters boarded at the home of Mr and Mrs Powell on Thompson Street and then moved into a cottage on the corner of George and Powell Streets. When land was donated they built a convent facing what is now the Hume Highway. This was a humble little building and was replaced in 1917.

St Joseph's Convent Bankstown NSW. c.1906.

During all this time, simmering below the surface, was the worry with regard to the Central Government which the majority of the Australian Bishops wished to have deleted from the Constitutions of the Sisters of St Joseph of the Sacred Heart. So in September 1887 Mary wrote to Dr Campbell of the Scots College, Rome at the direc-

---

9. *Freeman's Journal*, 21 September 1889, 17.
10. *Freeman's Journal*, 22 February 1890, 18.

tion of Mother Bernard, and begged him to use his 'kind influence and ask Father Bianchi to use his influence on behalf of the Central Government of the Institute'.[11] Mary was worried and anxious that the Bishops' representations to Rome would lead to the government of the congregation being made diocesan. Such had been their decision taken at their Synod. However as they were to learn, Rome did not accede to the bishops' demands.

Mary's beloved Uncle Donald McDonald died on 8 July 1887, and she was again in deep sorrow. He had been in failing health so she could accept his death as being a release from his pain and suffering and again she accepted God's will for her and could rejoice and give thanks for the wonderful life he had lived and the support he had been to her in those early days in Penola. He was buried in the cemetery attached to St Charles Church Ryde, next to his sister, Flora. His tombstone may still be seen there. Father Woods wrote to Mary on the death of this favourite uncle telling her that he was 'extremely sorry to hear of the death of your Uncle Donald, who was so dear to you . . . he acted to you in your early days like a father'.[12]

Mary cherished this letter from her beloved Father Founder as she still called him.

---

11. Mary MacKillop to Dr Campbell, 20 September 1887.
12. Father Woods to Mary MacKillop, 12 August 1887.

Chapter Seven
Many Foundations in 1888 and Good News from Rome

Rumours regarding the Bishops' determination to make the sisters into diocesan groups were a cause of worry to them. Some sisters thought that they would end up being diocesan and this had a disturbing effect, as the following story shows:

> You have heard, I suppose, that the Cardinal insisted upon Sisters M. Elizabeth and Aloysius' return, at least upon the latter's.[1] The Bishop of Brisbane wrote to them strongly condemning what they had done in violating their obedience and telling them to return. They came back, I hope, truly penitent and Sister Aloysius attributes her fall to listening first to uncharitable remarks and then joining in them, criticising Superiors' actions and arrangements, etc. They have made a good retreat.[2]

It seems that these two sisters, who were stationed at St Marys, had decided that they might be better off if they joined the diocesan group in Queensland, so the story has it that they left the key of the convent with the priest's housekeeper and set off.[3] With Mary's loving care they both regretted their rash act and remained to become useful sisters in the Congregation.

In March 1888 Mary was in Glen Innes when she received a letter from Mother Bernard who was in Kensington, South Australia. She was worried about business matters connected with the Industrial

---

1. Sister M Elizabeth Gunn and Sister Aloysius Ferricks.
2. Mary MacKillop to Sister Raymond Smyth, 8 March 1888.
3. Sheila McCreanor, *Mary MacKillop on Mission to Her Last Breath* (Sydney: Sisters of St Joseph, 2009), 135, fn. 103.

School soon to be opened at Elswick House in Leichhardt. This entailed much work and Mary was delegated to see to its organisation.

Mary had also to attend to the business associated with the sisters at Quirindi where in 1888 they succeeded the Lochinvar Sisters who had been established there. In 1887 that town was cut off from the Maitland Diocese and became part of Bishop Torreggiani's Diocese of Armidale. The diocesan Lochinvar Sisters of St Joseph vacated the convent and Bishop Torreggiani invited the Sisters of St Joseph of the Sacred Heart from North Sydney to replace them. He had previously asked for sisters for Casino but rearrangement of diocesan boundaries placed that town in the newly-created Lismore Diocese, so a change of plans was necessary. When they took charge of the school there were sixty-seven children on the roll. Sister Agnes Smith was the first superior. Quirindi then became the Provincial house for the sisters in the Armidale and Lismore dioceses.

During that year of 1888 the Sisters of St Joseph also arrived in Bungendore to open a school. The parish priest was Father E. Hanrahan. They resided for some time in a rented house opposite the church. This house had previously been a hotel, first known as 'Byrne's Inn' and later the 'Royal Hotel', before it became a private residence. School was conducted in a hall next door to the church. Following the usual practice the sisters put on a concert to raise money to pay for school furniture and other necessities.

Hall at Bungendore NSW. 2014. Door is from the original hall. Photo provided by Bernadette O'Sullivan rsj. Used with permission.

The *Goulburn Evening Penny Post* reported on one such event in its issue of 13 October 1888:

> For the past few weeks the Sisters of St Joseph's Convent School, Bungendore, have been busily engaged preparing the children attending their school to take part in a concert put up to aid in paying off the debt on the furniture of the above school.[4]

This concert was a great success and the sisters were assisted by Mary's cousin, Miss McDonald, who played all the accompaniments. Prominent among their supporters were Messrs N Colls and T McGrath, both of whom had daughters who became Sisters of St Joseph. Surprisingly, a second concert was put on in December of that same year and the object of this was 'to help the Sisters in paying off the debt on the piano and also assist in defraying their expenses to Sydney'.[5]

After the concert the hall was cleared and the adults danced until four o'clock in the morning, having supper at midnight! Such were the entertainments of the day. These country people enjoyed any excuse to dance the night away with their children sleeping soundly in various parts of the hall or perhaps joining in.

St Joseph's Convent Bungendore NSW. c.1906.

---

4. *Goulburn Evening Penny Post*, 13 October 1888, 6.
5. *Goulburn Evening Penny Post*, 15 December 1888, 3.

The business of the Leichhardt house being successfully concluded by Mary, on 3 May 1888, four Sisters of St Joseph took possession of a two-storey house in Renwick Street, and named it St Martha's Industrial Home. St Martha's became a home for children from single parent families where the mother had died and the father was unable to care for young children. The girls who came to St Martha's were trained in all forms of domestic work, cooking, laundry, dressmaking and domestic economy. Some of these young women learnt all forms of needlework, including lace making of all kinds so that when the time came, they were ready for employment.

Official opening of St Martha's Home Leichhardt NSW. 15 December 1889. Taken from collection of images in next photograph.

St Martha's Home Leichhardt NSW. Images taken at various times and published in 1906.

The Home became well known for its production of church vestments and all types of ecclesiastical sewing. Private orders were filled, for example, trousseau work for brides-to-be. School was provided for the girls who were of school age. When the time came such were their skills that most of the girls were able to find employment. Two of the sisters who opened St Martha's were Sister Augustine Brady, the first Superior, and Sister Regis O'Hare, who was sent to assist in the organisation and the financing for which she possessed great ability. Sister Regis spent the rest of her long religious life at St Martha's.

1888 was a busy year with new foundations and, with Mother Bernard in South Australia for much of the year, it was Mary who attended to the business associated with these. Back in March, Mother Bernard wrote to Mary from South Australia hoping that the business Mary had been asked to attend to in Glen Innes had been settled 'to everyone's satisfaction'.[6]

---

6. Mother Bernard to Mary MacKillop, 29 March 1888.

However, Mother Bernard did not always agree with changes that Mary made while she was away and wrote quite an angry letter to her in May disagreeing strongly with changes she had made at Villa Maria.[7] Mary had communicated her actions by letter and by telegram to Mother Bernard and the letter is a surprising one, coming as it did from Mother Bernard to the Foundress. The tension between the two was a cause of stress and anxiety for Mary. She had to obey the Mother General and yet she agonised over their differences of opinion with regard to various matters.

But for all the tensions and difficulties of that year, the close of 1888 brought wonderful news for the Sisters of St Joseph of the Sacred Heart and for Mary in particular, for Cardinal Moran brought to New South Wales the Decree that had been issued by Rome and dated 25 July. This Decree not only preserved Central Government but strengthened it. The Institution was erected into a Regular Congregation, those Bishops who wished, were permitted to constitute their houses into a diocesan Institute, and the Mother House, now to be in Sydney. The sisters in the diocesan Institutes were to make some alteration to their habits and their Rule.[8] Some Bishops decided not to alert their diocesan sisters to the choice that the decree had given them. Some found out about it many years later. This was the case of the sisters in the Wilcannia Diocese and at Bungaree in the Ballarat Diocese in Victoria.

One unfortunate decision, and one probably requested by Cardinal Moran, was that Mother Bernard was confirmed in office for a further ten years from the date of the Decree, 25 July 1888. The Decree also stated that after this date the election of the Superior General was to be made according to the Constitutions, that is, by a General Chapter.

Mary could write joyfully to the sisters about the Decree expressing her delight, and adding that 'this, my dearest Sisters, is a privilege I scarcely hoped to live to see though I never doubted about the Central Government'.[9]

---

7. Mother Bernard to Mary MacKillop, 9 May 1888.
8. Decree from the Sacred Congregation of Propaganda, given at Rome, 25 July 1888. Signed by John Cardinal Simeoni, Prefect.
9. Mary MacKillop to the sisters, 3 December 1888.

To Archbishop Reynolds she wrote at last in a long letter:

> I have said enough, perhaps too much, but my heart is full, and in writing to you tonight I can hardly realise that so many years have passed since I have written so freely to you. Then you were always my Bishop and Father. May I hope that, if I am still in disfavour with you, you will forgive my letter and kindly and generously help the Sisters. I know they won't give up Central Government. This is why I write to ask <u>you, their Archbishop and my old friend</u>, to tell them you do not mind the change of Mother House—that most of the Bishops are on this side and that they cannot find fault with the Mother House being in the Cardinal's city. Your Grace's own true heart will know what I mean and somehow I think you will understand me and not be displeased with this letter.[10]

Meanwhile back in August 1888 ceremonies had been held at Inverell and a report in the local paper stated that

> a procession was formed and his Lordship proceeded to the fine school attached to the convent of St Joseph . . . one of the finest and largest in the Diocese of Armidale.[11]

Just four months later *The Sydney Mail and New South Wales Advertiser* carried news that a severe storm had swept over the town and the convent school was completely demolished. When the NSW Department of Education refused to allow them to use a disused school, the sisters turned to others for help and the paper could make the statement that 'Messrs Wilson and Plumley have kindly placed the use of the Masonic Hall at the disposal of the Sisters. The school holds a very high standard for efficiency.'[12] The sisters taught for one more year at Inverell and then the school was passed on to the Grafton Sisters of Mercy.

The intransigency of Archbishop Reynolds in accepting the Decree was a constant worry to both Mother Bernard and Mary. Mother Bernard wrote several letters imploring the Archbishop to

---

10. Mary MacKillop to Archbishop Reynolds, 1 December 1888.
11. *Freeman's Journal*, 11 August 1888, 15.
12. *Sydney Mail and New South Wales Advertiser* (1860-1938), 22 December 1888, 1316.

give his answer regarding his position. The tone of one of these letters, written in January 1889, appears to have the style of Mary on whom Mother Bernard depended in business matters. In it she issued almost an ultimatum, reminding him:

> According to the Decree, the Sisters must do one thing or the other, that is, remain in South Australia united with the Mother House which the Holy See has transferred to Sydney—or, should Your Grace not consent to this and desire a diocesan community, then those who remain in unison with the Mother House here have no alternative but to leave South Australia, and this may God forbid.[13]

It took some intervention from Cardinal Moran for Archbishop Reynolds to finally agree to the conditions of the Decree.

Christmas of 1888 was a joyous one for Mary and the sisters for the news of the decree was a wonderful Christmas gift.

On 19 January 1889 the sisters were welcomed to Swan Bay on the Richmond River, a settlement in the new diocese of Grafton (later renamed Lismore) where the Bishop was Dr Jeremiah Joseph Doyle. The parish priest was Father Ahern and the ceremony of welcome on Sunday 13 January was reported as follows:

> He (Father Ahern) held in his hand an address of welcome to the good Sisters of the Order of St Joseph who had just arrived with the object of opening the Convent and carrying on the good work of educating the children.[14]

The sisters who arrived at Swan Bay were Sisters Casimir Meskill, Agatha Doherty, Justine Lupton and Petronella Whelan and they moved into the convent which was a compact six roomed cottage beside the church. On 13 December 1889 Bishop Doyle arrived by river steamer and confirmed forty children. The *Freeman's Journal* reported that

> His Lordship was highly pleased with the progress made by the children since the arrival of the Sisters, some eleven (11) months back . . . on the following day (Monday) the school

---

13. Mother Bernard to Archbishop Reynolds, 21 January 1889.
14. Northern Star (Lismore NSW: 1886 – 1954), 19 January 1889, 2.

was closed for the holidays. On the occasion of this event an entertainment was given by the pupils . . . a special mention should be made of the display of fancy work, which reflects great credit on the Sisters.[15]

The next day the sisters left by the steamer *Tomki* for Sydney.

In the ensuing years the sisters continued the work of educating the children and visiting the parishioners as well as taking the river boat twice a week to Coraki to teach the catholic children. They also took the riverboat to Woodburn, a distance of two and a half miles downstream, to educate the children there. Eventually they acquired a horse and buggy and this they put to good use visiting the parishioners and the parents of the children.

When Mother Bernard was in Kensington she wrote to Mary MacKillop telling her that she had received a letter from the Lismore Presentation sisters in which they mentioned that they expected a visit from the Swan Bay sisters. Mother Bernard went on to write:

> but I would wish they would stop at home and not be going about as I am sure it will not be the wish of the Bishop. Going about is what Dr Reynolds spoke of.[16]

Lismore was about thirty miles from Swan Bay and the steamers ran to Lismore regularly so this would have been a pleasant break for the sisters who lived in such an isolated place. Bishop Doyle would have been happy for them to visit the Lismore sisters.

The convent at Swan Bay was subject to flooding which meant that the sisters often had to be evacuated not to mention facing the threat of the snakes and other animals that came into the house with the flood waters. The sisters withdrew towards the end of 1894 following the tragic death of a young postulant, Sister Felicitas Pelley, who died on the way to Sydney by boat and was buried at Kempsey. The sisters had experienced an horrific flood and the young Postulant suffered shock which caused inflammation of the brain.[17]

---

15. Freeman's Journal, 28 January 1889, 10.
16. Mother Bernard to Mary MacKillop, 17 August 1889.
17. Kathleen Burford, *Unfurrowed Fields: A Josephite Story NSW 1872–1972* (North Sydney: St Joseph's Convent, 1991), 72.

The two sisters who accompanied the postulant to Sydney, Sisters Ambrosine O'Donnell and Hilary Toohey, did not return and the school was carried on by lay teachers. When a new school was built at Woodburn in 1933, the materials from the old church and school at Swan Bay were used. The report of the blessing and opening of this new school stated that the old Swan Bay convent

> had been occupied by the Sisters of St Joseph in their first foundation on the Richmond River. It was honoured on one occasion by a visit from Mother Mary MacKillop ... Many of the old men of the district who assisted in the construction of the new school were educated in the old Swan Bay convent.[18]

Those elderly men obviously remembered Mary's visit although it is uncertain when it actually took place.

Throughout 1889 Mary continued to guide the progress of the sisters in Sydney especially when Mother Bernard was in South Australia and the Industrial Home at Leichhardt was in the early stages of its ministry.

The third General Chapter of the Congregation was held from 18–20 December 1889. Since North Shore had become the Mother House of the Congregation by the Decree of 1888, the Chapter was held there and was presided over by Cardinal Moran. Mother Bernard had been re-appointed for ten years from the date of the Decree, so there was no election for a Mother General. At this Chapter it was decided that music could be taught by the sisters if necessary but there was a stipulation that a sister was not to teach music unless she had been examined by someone appointed by the Mother General and Council. The money provided by music teaching became necessary for the upkeep of the novitiates in Sydney and South Australia and, at this point, the paying off of the South Australian debt.[19]

From the time of the decision about the teaching of music, sisters with musical talent were prepared for music examinations. Annie MacKillop had a part in this and Mary, in a letter to Annie, told her that

---

18. *The Catholic Press*, 5 October 1933, 14.
19. The South Australian debt stood at more than £10,000.

> I am longing to hear how you got on with the examinations. Sr Monica in her last mentioned that Srs Teresa [Eickhoff] and Augustine [Woods] had been successful—I am so glad. Tell them so with my fond love.[20]

The following year she wrote to Sister Raymond that

> As Sr M. Anne [Forde] thinks Sr Augustine would pass Trinity College I think she might remain until Xmas.[21]

When the time came for the election of general councillors, Mary was elected as first councillor and thus maintained in the position of first assistant to Mother Bernard. Sister Josephine Carolan was elected as Provincial for Armidale although she had held the position during the past year, having been appointed by Mother Bernard.

At this Chapter the question of the Kensington Convent in South Australia was discussed and the Chapter decided to have it sold as the debt was great and the annual interest was a heavy burden on the sisters' resources.

The financial situation in Kensington weighed heavily on Sister Monica who was unable to keep up the interest on the mortgage. It was Mary who proposed a solution in sending Sister Veronica Champion, a business woman, to Adelaide to see what could be done. Mother Bernard was indecisive and could not make up her mind what to do, so Mary approached the Cardinal about the situation. Sister Veronica spent some time in South Australia and it looked as if the Kensington property was about to be sold. However, Archbishop Reynolds, who had an interest in the place, refused to allow the sale and so the property was saved and remained in the possession of the sisters.[22]

Father Woods died on 7 October 1889. Mary, who had succeeded in visiting him, was again attempting to visit him on that day but arrived at the house shortly after he died, as she wrote to Sisters Monica and Mechtilde Woods (his niece):

> I saw him about a fortnight before and then he said, 'It looks like the end but it's not'. It was so painful to see him and be of no use that after that I used to send and enquire but did not

---

20. Mary MacKillop to Annie MacKillop, 6 June 1898.
21. Mary MacKillop to Sister Raymond Smyth, 20 May 1899.
22. Foale, *Never see a Need*, 136–137.

care to go too often myself. They tell me he used to like a few strawberries. I tried now and then to send him some.[23]

She and the sisters were present at his requiem in St Mary's Cathedral and placed flowers on his coffin. Mary always reminded the sisters that he was their Father Founder and cherished his memory. How deeply she felt the rift between them and, in her saintly way, tried to bridge that gap.

---

23. Mary MacKillop to Sisters Monica and Mechtilde, October 1889.

Chapter Eight
The Years 1890–1892

In January 1890 Mary went with the Sisters to make the first Victorian foundation at Numurkah in the Sandhurst Diocese. From there she visited the sisters who had only recently arrived in Bacchus Marsh in the Melbourne Archdiocese and returned to Sydney on 23 February. Mary had made it a practice to send a circular letter to the sisters on a monthly basis. In her June letter she gave them news of her visit to the Armidale Province where she told them that in that Diocese:

> We have such nice convents and good schools. The Bishop is a great friend of the Sisters and does all he can to make them happy. I left here on Wednesday night and, between that and the Friday week following travelled 1090 miles and visited five convents and also paid a visit to the Bishop.[1]

All this she accomplished in about ten days. The five convents were those at Tenterfield, Inverell, Glen Innes, Uralla and Quirindi. Each visit entailed a thorough visitation of the sisters and their schools, as well as meeting with pastors and parishioners and the Bishop.[2]

Sister Josephine Carolan was the Provincial at this time and had had some problems with the defection of Sister M. Eugenius Raftery. Mary wrote of this in a letter to the sisters:

> I grieve to say that Sister M Eugenius, known to many of you, has proved unfaithful to her obligations and left her convent.

---

1. Mary MacKillop to the sisters, 2 June 1890.
2. In this context 'visitation' refers to the visit of Mary MacKillop, or another appointed by her, to the sisters in each convent.

> The Cardinal is shocked at the utter recklessness of some Sisters regarding the obligation of the vows.[3]

Mary exhorted the sisters to beware of pride, pride of intellect and self-will. She never lost an opportunity of using these examples to teach them and remind them of their responsibilities.

Later that year Mary visited Brisbane and, on 14 December 1890 from an address in Boundary Street South Brisbane, wrote her Christmas letter to the sisters in South Australia, beginning with: 'How strange it is that I should be writing my Christmas letter to you from Brisbane'.[4]

This was a very long letter exhorting them to remain true to their Constitutions. Mary mentioned the interruptions she had whilst writing, with visitors coming to see her. Were these the faithful friends of the late 1870s?

At Inverell, a concert organised by the sisters and held on 7 October 1890 played to a crowded house and was repeated the following night by special request.[5] Miss Cairns was the music teacher and accompanist on this occasion. This was their final concert since in January 1891, as *The Freeman's Journal* reported:

> In order to extend the blessings of Catholic education to the Catholic children of Tingha, his Lordship Dr Torreggiani arranged with the good Sisters of St Joseph to start a new little convent and school at Tingha. To supply the vacant place of Inverell, seven Sisters of Mercy were invited to go from Gunnedah to Inverell. In accordance with previous arrangements, the Gunnedah Sisters of Mercy, accompanied by the Bishop of the diocese, left Gunnedah on the 2nd and arrived in Inverell on the 7th of this month.[6]

This was 7 January 1891 and the Sisters of St Joseph had come to the end of their time at Inverell after a brief ten years. This allowed them to move on to Tingha. 1891 was to see new foundations at Tingha, Eden, Berry, Mittagong and Hillgrove.

---

3. Mary MacKillop to the sisters, 7 May 1890.
4. Mary MacKillop to the South Australian sisters, 14 December 1890.
5. *Australian Town and Country Journal*, 11 October 1890, 16.
6. *Freeman's Journal*, 17 January 1891, 18.

In January 1891 the newly named town of Berry, formerly called Broughton Creek, welcomed the sisters who arrived to establish a convent and school. Mary had been in correspondence with Father Harnett from before January 1885 as she had written in a PS to Archbishop Moran that she 'was forgetting to mention that we have not yet heard from Father Harnett about Broughton Creek'.[7]

It was six years later that the sisters came to live in the convent, a wooden six room cottage not far from the church. Mary visited Berry early in January. The school opened with eight pupils and Sister Sylvester Higgins was the first Superior. The number of pupils increased and when Mary visited the school in March 1899 there were thirty-seven children on the roll. The convent became the catholic centre for the young town as the parish priest resided at Nowra.

St Joseph's Convent Berry NSW. c.1906.

When the convent and school were opened in the little tin-mining town of Tingha in January, Mary accompanied the sisters from Sydney, as the newspaper of the day reported:

---

7. Mary MacKillop to Archbishop Moran, 20 January 1885.

On Wednesday morning, 21st January, three Sisters, accompanied by the Rev. Mother Mary of the Cross, founder of the Order of the Sisters of St Joseph, arrived at Guyra from Sydney by train. At Guyra station the Sisters found the mail coach ready to take them to Tingha. On the arrival of the coach in Tingha at about 9.00 p.m. the Bishop with many people from the town received the Sisters with great cheers. On Monday, being a public holiday, the Sisters took down the names of the children who intended to attend their school and on Tuesday morning 27th January they opened the school with 44 children. In due course they will have about 100. Catholics, Protestants, and Chinese promise to assist the good Sisters.[8]

Another newspaper account mentioned that the sisters passed through Paradise where the people entertained them to afternoon tea with

> the best refreshments they had in store. However enchanted with the beauty of Paradise, the Sisters left it and continued on their journey to Tingha.[9]

St Joseph's Convent Tingha NSW. c.1906.

---

8. *Advocate*, 14 February 1891, 9.
9. *Freeman's Journal*, 31 January 1891, 17. Paradise is the name of a small town between Guyra and Tingha.

The convent consisted of six rooms and a detached kitchen and refectory and was the sisters' own property. After settling the sisters in Tingha, Mary proceeded to Glen Innes where, in March, she wrote to all the sisters a letter to mark the Silver Jubilee of the Congregation. It was a time for Mary to reflect on the past and give thanks to God for the blessings of those twenty-five years. She wrote:

> Twenty-five years ago we first kept up St Joseph's day as the special feast of our proposed Institute and little did either of us then dream of what was to spring from so small a beginning ... Our poor Father was happy that day and so was I, but we said little beyond wondering whom God would call to assist us—and how He would make His way clear ... God has done wonders for us ... pray to be worthy children of St. Joseph's great Institute—pray to have the true spirit of the same—that prosperity may not elate, nor adversity ever shake your courage and generosity in the service of God.[10]

Mary wrote from her own life experience as she, in the quiet of the convent at Glen Innes, pondered on those twenty-five momentous years. Was she thinking of all that she had experienced in those years, of the adversities she had undergone and the good that had come out of what had seemed disasters? Was she recalling her father's warning to her in her childhood, about being elated at success and discouraged at defeats and disappointments?[11] Mary had learned the lesson of courage and generosity in God's service. She wanted her sisters to be courageous and generous women.

Eden, too, welcomed the sisters in 1891. The link with Eden was established in 1886 when the *Ly-ee-Moon* sank on the Green Cape reef on 30 May 1886. Mary was always grateful for the way the residents of Eden cared for her Mother's body when it was rescued from the sea. A Catholic woman, Mrs Power, seeing the scapulars on the body, asked to be given care of it and she and a midwife, Emma Strangwidge, did so. The remains were conveyed to the Hotel owned by Mr and Mrs Power where the body was placed in their best room. The two ladies reverently laid it out and surrounded it with flowers and lights until it was placed in the coffin.[12]

---

10. Mary MacKillop to the sisters, 6 March 1891.
11. *Resource Material*, Issue No 2, August 1983, 9.
12. Bernadette O'Sullivan, *Flora MacKillop A Truly Blessed Mother* (Homebush, Sydney: St Paul's Publications, 2012), 164.

On 10 August 1891 Father Sheridan welcomed three sisters at the Eden wharf—Sisters Joseph Mary Fitzgerald, Mary de Sales O'Brien and Beatrice Mulvihill. A small rented cottage close to the Church was occupied by the sisters until a suitable convent was built behind the Church. School was conducted in the small wooden church which had been built in the 1860s. Here the sisters taught classes at either end of the building and they did this for many years.

St Joseph's Convent Eden NSW. c.1906.

The convent was soon completed and on 20 September Bishop Higgins blessed and opened the building which cost £600. The *Freeman's Journal* reported the event and concluded it by saying that

> the Sisters of St. Joseph are in charge of the convent and school, and already those silent, collected, but impressive ladies have made their teaching and the influence of their good example felt in our midst.[13]

The following year when Bishop Higgins visited Eden for Confirmation, the same Journal provided an interesting snippet:

> The church, which is looked after by the good Sisters of St. Joseph, was most tastefully decorated, and the word 'Welcome' was most artistically worked in flowers. His Lordship expressed himself greatly pleased with the decorations.[14]

---

13. *Freeman's Journal*, 10 October 1891, 17.
14. *Freeman's Journal*, 5 November 1892, 15.

The sisters also provided boarding facilities for some of the children from outlying areas who could not make the daily trip into school.

The Dominican Sisters took charge of the Moss Vale School in 1891, enabling the Sisters of St Joseph to open a convent and school at Mittagong. Initially they occupied a small cottage in Arthur Street opposite the school grounds.

Students, Sisters, Mittagong NSW. 1912.

A local newspaper had an interesting event to report in February 1892:

> During the past week a sensation has been caused by some persons throwing stones at St Joseph's Convent, Mittagong, serious alarm being occasioned to the Sisters thereby. The Convent to some extent is secluded, being surrounded by bush, although several neighbours live close by, and it was a difficult matter to find out the person who was committing these dastardly outrages. However, the police on Wednesday discovered that two tramps were the cause of the disturbance, and they were arrested. The Sisters, not prosecuting, they were let off.[15]

The foundation stone of a new convent was laid on 2 September 1900 when Father Sheridan was parish priest. Monsignor O'Brien, representing the Cardinal, laid the stone and Father Sheridan presented him with a silver trowel.[16]

---

15. *Bowral Free Press and Berrima District Intelligence*, 20 February 1892, 2.
16. *Freeman's Journal*, 8 September 1900, 12.

The other foundation made in 1891 was that at Hillgrove, near the Baker's Creek gold mine, where the sisters found the church, school and convent already built of weatherboard. Bishop Torregiani and Dean O'Connor had visited Hillgrove in March of that year and the people agreed to build the convent. The *Freeman's Journal* reported in September that

> The Convent at Hillgrove was opened on Sunday last by the Very Rev. Dean O'Connor . . . The school was opened on Monday by three of the Sisters of St Joseph, with an attendance of seventy, which it is expected will soon amount to 150. We heartily wish the good Sisters success.[17]

The convent was ready for the sisters when they arrived in late August or early September. Sr Agnes Smith was one of the pioneer sisters at Hillgrove and year after year their successful concerts, bazaars, picnics, music examinations and scholastic successes were reported in great detail in the newspapers of the day. When the Bishop visited later that year he was very pleased to see that the enrolment had grown to 114. By October 1892 there were 170 pupils taught by five sisters. The sisters accepted children not of the catholic faith as the gold mines attracted people of many denominations who wanted an education for their children.

St Joseph's Hillgrove NSW.

---

17. *Freeman's Journal*, 12 September 1891, 19.

Mary had long desired to have a chapel built as a memorial to Father Julian Tenison Woods. She had written of it in her Jubilee letter where she expressed her fond wish and hope

> that we shall be able to start the building of our Oratory—the Mother House Chapel, dedicated to St. Joseph in memory of our departed Father. I feel sure that God will bless us in this and send us the means of building it without incurring fresh debt; pray that we may succeed and that we may have a Chapel worthy, as far as becomes us, of our Glorious Patron, and of our dear Father's memory.[18]

This chapel was built during 1891 and on Sunday, 13 December 1891, Cardinal Moran blessed and opened the building. According to the report in the *Sydney Morning Herald* on Monday 14 December:

> A marble slab on the front of the Chapel bears the following inscription: 'Memorial Chapel erected to commemorate the Silver Jubilee of the congregation of the Sisters of St Joseph of the Sacred Heart, Blessed and dedicated to St. Joseph by his Eminence Cardinal Moran, December 13 1891.' After the religious ceremony had been performed the visitors assembled in the new building. Cardinal Moran presided.[19]

Marble slab on the front of the Tenison Woods Conference Centre, Mary MacKillop Place North Sydney NSW. 2017. Photo provided by Bernadette O'Sullivan rsj. Used with permission.

---

18. Mary MacKillop to the sisters, 6 March 1891.
19. *Sydney Morning Herald*, 14 December 1891, 8.

Although the building is no longer used as a chapel, this marble slab may still be seen on the front of the building. Sadly, Mary was not present for the opening as she was very ill in Melbourne where she had been supervising the setting up and working of the Children's Home at Surrey Hills and moving extensively around Victoria visiting the children who had been fostered out. As well she had attended to the opening of the Providence in Melbourne.

At the end of 1891 she was thought to be dying. Months of illness followed, her life was despaired of but she gradually recovered and the Archbishop of Melbourne arranged for her to go to suburban Sandringham to recuperate. It was a long convalescence through the early months of 1892 and her doctor wanted her to remain under his care until she was fully recovered but Mother Bernard needed her back in Sydney. Reluctantly the doctor had to agree but he arranged for her to leave the train at Wagga and rest in the home of a friend of his, another doctor. This she and Sister Ethelburg Job, her nurse, did but she was so ill that she had to remain there for some time and then had to leave the train again at Bungendore where she remained until she was strong enough to return to North Sydney, which was not until July 1892, three months after she had set out.[20] As the Bungendore convent had been blessed and opened in September 1891, this was where she convalesced.

It was mid-July before she was able to move about. She began a round of duties that she described in a letter to Sister Annette Henschke in Adelaide. These included visiting the Orphanage, Gosford, Lithgow, Penrith and other places. She told Annette that a lot of work had fallen to her. As well as that she was busy preparing a Confirmation class at Mossman's Bay. No wonder she had not been able to write.[21] Previously she had written to Annette from St Martha's Home where she was preparing for the visit of Lady Duff from Government House.[22]

When she wrote to Sisters Annette and Bernardine Ledwith on 21 October she was able to tell them her reason for going to Lithgow. It was to help with

---

20. Joan Ryan, *A Seed is Sown, The History of the Sisters of St Joseph of the Sacred Heart, 1890-1920* (Melbourne: Advent Business Forms, 1992), 60.
21. Mary MacKillop to Sister Annette Henschke, 7 September 1892.
22. Mary MacKillop to Sister Annette Henschke, 1 August 1892.

> getting up a concert in aid of the convent funds there, which took place on Sept 16th and then doing a little begging with Sister M Josephine up the Mountains for the same purpose, then home to get up the Guardian Angels Feast, then down to the Orphanage on 8th for the meeting there of the Cardinal, the Bishop of Sale, and a lot of priests and laymen.[23]

It must be remembered that Mary was a capable musician and was fond of singing. Her efforts at training children for a concert would have been something to see. Not only did she work with the children but she persuaded Madame Merz, Miss Josephine O'Reilly, Mr E Finn, Miss Emily Finn and Miss McGrath, all of whom had beautiful voices, to come from Sydney to assist. The concert was presented to an appreciative audience in a crowded hall. The *Freeman's Journal* reported the event in its issue of 1 October 1892.[24] The report also mentioned that these artists sang at the Mass and Benediction the following Sunday. Whatever Mary did, she ensured that events such as concerts and bazaars were of the highest standard and she was not afraid to call on men and women of talent to assist her.

At Cooranbong a new convent was blessed by Cardinal Moran on 5 November 1892. This was a two-storey building and cost £400. The pastor of the district was Rev. Father O'Reilly.[25] It is probable that Mary attended this event.

She visited Lithgow again from 8–22 November 1892 then went on to Gosford and Kincumber returning to Sydney at the end of November. Back at North Sydney she was busy with Christmas and the Retreat.

---

23. Mary MacKillop to Sisters Annette and Bernardine, 27 October 1892.
24. *Freeman's Journal*, 1 October 1892, 15.
25. *Freeman's Journal*, 12 November 1892, 14.

Chapter Nine
Events of 1893–1895

There were no new foundations in the year 1893 and Mary spent the year in and around the North Shore. She wrote a very long circular letter to the sisters on St Joseph's Day. In it she extolled the virtues of Saint Joseph, the fruit of her own meditations. In this letter she asked the sisters to

> Consider who we are; what we are doing here; in what relation we stand towards this great Saint, and consequently the obligation under which we are placed of imitating his virtues.[1]

She went on to answer these questions in the light of her own reflections, then reminded the sisters of his virtues.

In June she wrote to her good friend Sister Annette and told her that she had been very ill and that when she was better she had so many things to attend to that she was out every day and was too tired to write to anyone. She mentioned that she was so often from home that she could not keep track of her letters. She wrote about the forthcoming Retreat:

> There was some talk of not having any this midwinter unless such as I could read out to the young Sisters—<u>this</u> because there was no money. However, the Jesuits are my dear tried friends. I let the Provincial know our difficulty and he <u>at once</u> said we should have Fr Power if we wished, though he had intended him to give a Retreat elsewhere at the time we want him. May God bless and reward the Jesuits.[2]

---

1. Mary MacKillop to the sisters, 19 March 1893.
2. Mary MacKillop to Sister Annette Henschke, 3 June 1893.

She was concerned about two Aboriginal boys whom Father Donald had brought with him from the Northern Territory. Whilst he was on his begging tour to raise funds for the mission Mary offered to care for the boys at St Marys.

She wrote:

> We are keeping the black boys at St Marys, near Penrith, but he (Donald) is paying 10/- a week for them. He could not get a pass for them on the railway, and had not money to pay travelling expenses, besides, neither of them is strong, and they want care and warmth in the winter.[3]

In this letter she also wrote of the illness of Archbishop Reynolds and the Masses and prayers she was having said for him. She wrote that sometimes she had thought of writing to him but feared that she might do him more harm than good by doing so.[4]

Archbishop Reynolds died on 12 June 1893 and Mary grieved that the friendship that she had treasured in the early days of the congregation had turned to bitterness on his part and that any communication from her would not be welcome. Mary, however, harboured no such ill-will and had many Masses and prayers said for him.

In a letter written at that time to Sister Monica she asked her to send

> a list of the different convents in your Province, and the names of the Sisters in each. I must try to write to them after the Retreat, at least to most of them. Have you any idea what convent sent me back the circular I sent for St Joseph's Day? The wrapper had an Adelaide stamp and was posted evidently in Adelaide, but whatever Sister sent it, she cut out the name of the convent to which I had in the first place directed it. It was a pity that she had not the courage to let me know who she was. I sent one of the circulars to every convent in the Archdiocese of Adelaide, with writing such as I put on yours and others you may have seen. I have my suspicions of where it came from, but it must have been, in that case, sent to someone in Adelaide to post.[5]

---

3. Mary MacKillop to Sister Annette Henschke, 3 June 1893.
4. Mary MacKillop to Sister Annette Henschke, 3 June 1893.
5. Mary MacKillop to Sister Monica Phillips, 4 June 1893.

What a treasure that circular would have been for the sisters in that convent. They did not realise what they had missed. Mary was hurt by the rejection but was not bitter. What had she done to cause such pettiness?

Mary was continually busy in spite of being almost crippled with rheumatism. In November she was again at Lithgow for a week helping the sisters prepare for Bishop Higgins' visit for Confirmation. She was there, too, for a fundraising bazaar opened by the Bishop for church funds.[6]

After the bazaar Mary went to Gosford to help the priest prepare for Confirmation. The children, she said, were really wild with ignorance. After the ceremony she moved to Kincumber for a little peace and quiet. In a letter to Sister Monica she told her that

> MG expects to have to go to Court next week. God help Mother Bernard if she is put in the witness box, and pity help us all. It is a question about the Orphanage and a debt contracted for building, and if not settled out of Court, will, I fear, go against M. Bernard. If the Cardinal were home, he might help her out of it. As it is nothing but prayer will do.[7]

Mary had feared that the Orphanage would pass into other hands but prayer did prevail and the Orphanage and the sisters continued their wonderful work.

The school at Menangle which had opened in 1885 experienced a decline in enrolments and the sisters withdrew at the end of 1893.

Mary reported to Sister Annette in January 1894 that she had never been in better health, that the past terrible attacks had ceased. She had been extremely busy in the past months and was about to make her first visit to the sisters in New Zealand. In spite of pleas from the New Zealand sisters, Mother Bernard had never made the trip and now sent Mary. She was away from January 1894 until March 1895 and accomplished much during her stay there.

Whilst Mary was away in New Zealand the Bondi school was opened:

---

6. Mary MacKillop to her cousin John MacKillop, 9 November 1893.
7. Mary MacKillop to Sister Monica Phillips, 27 November 1893.

> In 1894 the Sisters of St Joseph opened their first school at Bondi in a small two-roomed cottage, 32 Penkivil Street, and they travelled by tram daily from the Providence in Cumberland Street.[8]

What was not added was that the tram only went as far as Bondi Junction. Did the sisters walk the rest of the way to Penkivil Street, a considerable distance of about one and a half kilometres?

The sisters also opened a school at Naremburn in 1894. This school was often mentioned in Mary's diary but she called it 'Central Township' and the sisters travelled there by tram from Mount Street until a convent opened in 1912.

When she returned from New Zealand in March 1895, she told the New Zealand Sisters that whilst she was away

> MG and SM Veronica are having great improvements made to the convent—the two houses knocked into one by the dividing wall in the passage of the two front houses being taken down, making one large entrance hall. The division between the verandah and balconies is also taken down, making one long verandah and balcony in front. The old fence in front is taken away and a brick wall built instead. All will be very nice when finished.[9]

Mary took up her duties with a constant round of visits, in between bouts of illness, to Camperdown, Leichhardt, The Providence, St Martha's Leichhardt, Annandale, Mossman's Bay, Granville, Kincumber, St Bridget's School, Rookwood (Lidcombe) and Central Township (Naremburn) in the city. Visits were also made to country places such as Bulli, Kiama, and Camden. She also made a quick visit to Quirindi in early December.

Not long after she arrived home from New Zealand, Mary, who was constantly writing letters, often business ones for Mother Bernard, mentioned in her diary on 29 March that she had written to the sisters at the Barbadoes Street convent in New Zealand where she stayed whilst in Christchurch. Did she take the opportunity to visit the Barbadoes Street Cemetery where her brother, John MacKillop, was buried?

---

8. Burford, *Unfurrowed Fields*, 66.
9. Mother Mary to the New Zealand sisters, 15 March 1895.

In the midst of all her busyness during this early part of 1895, Mary took a day off to accompany Sister M Collette and the Providence children to Rose Bay where the sisters and children there gave these children a treat and also paid for the omnibus to transport the visitors who arrived home at a quarter to seven in the evening.[10]

On 20 April 1895 Mary travelled to Cooranbong where she was met by Mr Healy. The priests at that time were Fathers Coen and O'Shea. The sisters at Cooranbong were too poor to pay the fare of Sister Alphonsus who travelled back to Sydney with Mary. On her return to the North Shore, Mary took up the duties of Little Sister. She was concerned about Sister Columba whom she visited many times in hospital and who finally had to be transferred to the Gladesville Asylum. Mary's comment was that all were very sad and that it was worse than having a death in the house. By this time there was a telephone installed in the house at Mount Street and Mary used it to ask for news of Sister Columba. Sister Columba left the Congregation at a later date.

Mary's compassionate heart grieved for any of her sisters who fell ill. One example of her care was the story told by Sister Bridget Healy. She wrote:

> I am under a great debt of gratitude to her (Mary) for all her kindness to me when I was dying. How she minded me in her own room for over a fortnight. She used to get up at four o'clock in the morning and beat up an egg for me.[11]

Mary's diary for 1895 reads like a travelogue as she recorded her daily doings. She went into town on many occasions, sometimes twice a day, she visited the hospital, St Marys, Camperdown, St Brigid's to distribute medals, Parramatta, Rookwood, Redfern, to St Vincent's Hospital and a two night visit to Cooranbong from 18 May. Always she seemed to be conducting business, writing letters, and attending council meetings with Mother Bernard. Mary found some of these council meetings very painful as she also noted in her diary.

A new sanctuary and vestry were added to the western end of the Tenison Woods' Chapel and Mary was responsible for organising this: calling and accepting tenders, as well as overseeing the builder

---

10. Mary MacKillop's Diary, 1895.
11. Sister Bridget Healy to Sister La Merci Mahony, 15 August 1909.

who started work on 1 July 1895. When the work was finished in September she was busy preparing the new sanctuary and vestry for the blessing and opening for which she wrote the invitations herself. The Cardinal performed the ceremony on Sunday, 13 October. Two sisters, Idus McNamara and Gerard Rowan, were professed on that day.

Mary visited the convent at Bungendore with Mother Bernard on 10 July 1895. They had gone to Goulburn to meet with Archbishop O'Reily, the newly appointed Archbishop of Adelaide, but he had already left. Some of Mary's MacKillop relatives, drove them to see various places in Goulburn. Then they went to Bungendore where Mary saw more of the MacKillop family. At the convent they found the sisters all working happily. Mary started for Sydney at night with Mother Bernard and Sister M Ignatius accompanying her as far as Tarago. Presumably, Mother Bernard stayed on at Bungendore for a few days. The railway had been extended to Tarago in January 1884 and to Bungendore in March 1885.

In many places that Mary visited, she found relatives—either MacKillops or McDonalds—and these she visited, too. Many of these in New South Wales country places were mentioned in her diary. MacKillops were to be found in Goulburn, Kiama and Terra Bella Station (near Wellington) where there were descendants of her father's brother, Uncle Duncan MacKillop. Then there were McDonalds in Nimitybelle and Stanthorpe in Queensland (not far from Tenterfield), and all were acknowledged and often were the recipients of her begging letters for funds for the sisters' Institutions.

Typical of Mary's zeal was the note in her diary of how she prepared the Garvan children for their First Communion at Central Township (Naremburn). How well they were prepared for this and for their First Confession and one can be sure of the trouble she took to have a little breakfast for them after that Mass on the Feast of the Assumption— Mary's favourite feast. When their mother wrote to thank Mary she enclosed two guineas. She immediately used it to pay the doctor's bills.[12] One of these bills was for Sister Columba for whom Mary was taking special care.

Mary fitted in a visit to Kiama, stayed overnight and on the way home she called at Bulli where she remained for two hours before taking the train to Sydney. On 20 September Father Buckeridge said

---

12. Mary MacKillop's Diary, 8–15 August 1895.

the first Mass in the new sanctuary for Mary's intentions. The following day the sisters moved furniture into the new vestry and the old vestry became the chapter room. That 22 September Mary recalled was the twenty-fourth anniversary of the excommunication. What memories stirred in her and how she gave thanks to God for all the blessings of those twenty-four years.

Before 1895 came to a close, on 6 December, Mary was again at Quirindi. When Sister Josephine Carolan was Provincial and living at Quirindi, the convent was in such disrepair, she saw the need for a new building. So she bought a block of land on the opposite side of the road and the new convent was built and owned by the sisters.[13]

St Joseph's Convent Quirindi NSW. c.1906.

When it was opened on Sunday, 7 November 1895, Mary was present, having been sent by Mother Bernard. She left Sydney on Friday evening, 6 November, by the six-fifteen evening Mail Train, arriving at Quirindi at two-thirty the next morning. She helped the sisters prepare for the bishop who arrived on Saturday evening. Mary wrote in her diary that the convent was blessed with great fanfare. Prior Vaughan OP preached and the collection amounted to £53.

---

13. Sister Josephine Carolan to Mary MacKillop, 13 May 1905.

This was a great day and Mary was pleased that the appeal for funds was so successful. On the return journey she called at the Kincumber Orphanage before returning to Sydney.

The year 1895 saw the closure of the convent at West Kempsey, so strangely opened in 1884 when Kempsey included in its territory the whole of the Macleay River district. Years later a newspaper article could report:

> Owing to the isolated situation of the parish, and the great difficulties of communication with their Mother House, the Sisters of St Joseph having accomplished excellent work, were obliged to relinquish both the convent and school at Kempsey. A community of Presentation Nuns, with Mother M. Ignatius Barnewall as Superior, then arrived in Kempsey. The same set of circumstances made it impossible for them to remain for any length of time. In 1900 the Sisters of Mercy took charge of the school at Kempsey.[14]

So, at last, Sisters of Mercy came to Kempsey after the debacle of 1884.

Mary MacKillop. c.1890.

---

14. *Freeman's Journal*, 17 June 1937, 36.

Chapter Ten
A Round of Visits

In Mary's diary for 5 January 1896 she mentioned that at the end of the Retreat 'both priests came out to the grotto which Father Coue blessed, after which the sisters sang a hymn'.[1]

This grotto of Our Lady of Lourdes was built on the site of the first novitiate, a one-storey wooden building adjacent to Alma Cottage, a building used as a practice school for the novices. Later the grotto was moved to the end of the back yard and, later still, was demolished to make room for new buildings.

An example of Mary's horsemanship appears in a diary entry later in the month after she had experienced a bout of illness. She described how she drove Father's buggy and Waterhouse's good horse out to Military Road (Mossman) with Sister Frances Xavier Amsinck. She loved having the reins in her own hands and her prowess with borrowed horses and buggies rated many mentions in her diaries, whether it was around the city of Sydney or to Penrith or further afield.

Mother Bernard wanted Mary to go to Bulli where there had been a falling-off in school attendance. So she left on 24 January and spent some days there, visiting the school and questioning the fall-off in attendance. She had a discussion with Father Barlow who agreed to allow lay teachers to open at Helensburgh provided that Flora (McDonald), her cousin, was the leading one. After many discussions and meetings with Father Barlow this did not happen and the Helensburgh convent and school did not open until May 1900. Father

---

1. Mary MacKillop's Diary, 5 January 1896.

Barlow moved from parish to parish and he was mentioned in several diary entries.

In 1896 the sisters took charge of St Columba's School at Leichhardt North. They travelled there daily from St Martha's, Renwick Street, as did the sisters who taught at St Fiacre's School until they moved to a cottage in Catherine Street.

In the early part of 1896 Mary's diary showed how busy she was arranging picnics, visiting sick sisters, attending to accounts and other business matters. This entailed much activity and she often came home very tired. She was also preparing for the General Chapter which took place from 19–21 March. Mary was again elected to the General Council as first assistant to the Mother General.

On 26 March she visited Camden, Mittagong and Picton. She continued with her round of visits until she set out for the Armidale Province on 18 April for Visitation. At the Fourth General Chapter, Sister Josephine McMullen was elected as Provincial of the Armidale Province, replacing Sister Josephine Carolan who was appointed Superior of the Mother House.[2] The Armidale Provincial House up to this time at Quirindi, was transferred to Uralla. On 18 April, using a free rail pass, Mary set out. She reached Quirindi at seven o'clock in the evening feeling very tired. Sisters Pauline Wilson and M. Rose met her at the station. A parish Mission was taking place so next day she went with Sister Pauline to visit some Catholics who were not attending.[3] She visited and examined the school and was very pleased with the children. She waited at Quirindi to see the Bishop who arrived on Thursday, 23 April and after her meeting with him she caught the mail train to Tamworth where she stayed overnight with the Dominican Sisters and returned to Quirindi the next day. She made no mention in her diary of the reason for this visit to Tamworth but it is likely that it was in connection with a begging tour seeking funds to pay off the debt on the Quirindi convent. The Mission concluded on Sunday when the bishop confirmed a great many candidates. She gave an instruction to the sisters and did not go to bed as she had to start at two o'clock next morning for Uralla.

---

2. The Mother House is the main convent for the whole Congregation.
3. A Parish Mission is a time of renewal of the parish when the community gather to listen to dynamic speakers who encourage them to live out their faith.

Her written report showed that there were eighty-four children on the roll and she examined seventy-eight. There were fourteen music pupils and two boarders. The community comprised Sisters Mary Agnes Smith, Mary Rose Lehane, Cuthbert Williams, Pauline Wilson and Julian Griffin. The convent was comfortably furnished and the sisters were happy and trying hard to pay off the building debt.

Mary arrived at Uralla at seven o'clock and was met by Maggie Brennan who brought her to the convent in a bus. What was a bus in those days, one wonders?[4] Uralla had been open for ten years and now the community consisted of Sister Josephine McMullen, the newly-appointed Provincial, Sisters Benigna Hammersley, Donatus Kreutzer and two postulants. When Sister Josephine arrived at the end of March she found the convent destitute of house linen. Sister Benigna had discovered old debts which she was paying off by degrees.[5] Mary noted that the house was plainly furnished. One of her chief concerns when she visited the sisters was to see that they had warm clothing and good boots in these cold climates and that their beds were good and warm. She was sure to remedy any of these necessities. Poverty was important but not destitution.

Here, too, she visited some Catholics who were encouraged to take up their religious duties. On 29 April she examined the school where there were eighty-seven children enrolled and she was very pleased both with the children and the school. At recreation with the sisters she played dominoes for the first time! She obviously was delighted with this simple game and when she visited other convents purchased the game and taught it to the sisters. On her way to Glen Innes she stayed overnight at the Armidale convent after she had visited some people that she knew. Mary seemed to have contacts in many places and went out of her way to visit people who had been kind to the sisters and herself.

On Friday, 1 May she left by the quarter past eight mail train for Glen Innes having been driven to the railway in Mr Madden's trap. Modern readers might ask what was a trap.[6] She arrived at Glen Innes at one-thirty having sorted her letters on the train, and was met by

---

4. See Appendix 3.
5. Sister Benigna Hammersley lived at Uralla for ten years and then was appointed to Glen Innes in June 1905. She attended the 1905 General Chapter of the Congregation held in March.
6. See Appendix Three for a definition of a 'trap.'

Sisters Blandina O'Donnell and Julia Donnelly. She had a busy afternoon, visited the school, met with Fathers Gibbons and O'Donoghue and attended devotions in the Church in the evening.

The sisters made her a new veil and for this, Father Gibbons cut out the cardboard! They also gave her some wool for her knitting. On Sunday afternoon Mary took the sisters for a drive using Mr Porter's horse and buggy. When they visited Mrs Wynne she promised to have Mary and Sister M. Margaret Crowe driven to Inverell on their way to Tingha. On Tuesday she examined the school where there were 140 children enrolled and she examined ninety-nine of them and was very pleased with all of them. There were five Sisters at Glen Innes: Sisters Blandina O'Donnell, M Margaret Crowe, Julia Donnelly, Anselm Hyland and a Postulant. All spoke highly of Sister Blandina as their Little Sister and all were happy.[7] Although the convent was owned by the parish, the sisters were hoping to paint the outside. They owned the piano, sewing machine, harmonium and furniture.

Once again Mary ensured that the sisters had good food and beds. The pastor was kind and did not interfere in any way. If he had cut out the cardboard for Mary's new veil, he obviously was on good terms with the sisters and enjoyed this simple task.

An interesting note on the report mentioned that Sister M Margaret told Mary that her mother had given her the full amount and more to cover the cost of her new teeth and that she had given it to Mother Bernard to pay the dentist. Mary knew that Mother Bernard had not paid the account but did not tell the sister—an example of something that Mary would have to remedy.

She went by train from Glen Innes to Tenterfield on Wednesday, 6 May. Her knitting was not progressing because she had run out of wool on the journey and had to write to Sister Blandina for more. Knitting seems to have been one of Mary's favourite occupations. She learnt a new stitch from Sister Lucy Crowley when she was in Adelaide in August 1896.[8]

At Tenterfield there were three sisters: Camillus O'Brien, Killian Allen and F. de Sales Connolly. In this convent they had a poor orphan child whom they kept without assistance and an elderly lady,

---

7. A 'Little Sister' was the Sister appointed to take charge of a particular religious community.
8. Mary MacKillop Diary, 17 August 1896.

Mrs Mooney, who occupied a room off the verandah. She was very helpful to the sisters.

On Thursday Mary examined the school pupils all day and was delighted with them. As she had not completed the school examination she did this the next day and gave the children a holiday and some lollies. There were 123 children on the roll. On Saturday and Sunday she had a great number of callers, among them Mrs Nora McDonald from Stanthorpe in Queensland who was disappointed that her husband, Sergeant Alexander McDonald, could not come.

Once again she checked to see that the sisters had warm clothing and good boots with warm stockings. The convent itself was greatly in need of painting and the bishop had given the sisters permission to get money for this in any way they could and the parish priest, Father Corcoran, consented also. Why wouldn't he? He probably knew that the sisters were good fundraisers. Mary left a very happy and united community and made her way to Glen Innes on the early morning train.

She was in time to see the children at Pole Drill which she thought was splendid. The next day, as arranged, Tom Wynne came and started with her for Inverell in terrible thunder and a hail storm. She reached Inverell drenched and cold. She stayed with Father English and his house-keeper, Miss Keating, and attended May devotions. After breakfast and a visit to the Sisters of Mercy (who had taken charge of the Inverell convent and school when the Sisters of St Joseph left in 1890), Father English and Miss Keating, his cousin, drove her to Tingha, a distance of fifteen miles.

Mary recalled that she had brought the sisters to Tingha five years previously when the convent opened. After dinner she visited the school with Father English and the children sang a Scotch song for her. She examined the school on Friday, 15 May, and was very pleased with the children. There were sixty-five children on the roll. She also went out visiting and had a happy evening with Sisters Lucy O'Neill, M Ambrose Ryan and Gregory Kain. The convent, which consisted of six rooms and a detached kitchen and refectory, was their own property as were all the contents including the sacred vessels in the chapel. Mary noted that the house was poor and everything in it was poor, but clean. She found the sheeting and the sisters' underclothing well-worn and patched—something she immediately remedied. She did note that they had warm clothing and good boots. When there was no Mass the sisters said the Rosary with the children and Mary encouraged them to stir up the parents to attend.

Sister Lucy O'Neill recalled this visit many years later and had a story to tell:

> Mother Mary came to visit us once in Tingha. She had driven some miles in a snow storm, but her first wish was to visit the school. There was a poor little barefoot ragged boy standing in the class. Mother went straight to him and putting her arms around him she kissed him saying, 'Ah Sister, these are the children I love'.[9]

This was typical of Mary's love for the poor and especially the children of the poor.

Mary, in her report, made mention of the music teacher who had eight pupils. She was paid five pounds per quarter. Music fees amounted to eight pounds eight shillings per quarter. School fees per week were ten shillings and a penny halfpenny. The sisters paid their household bills as they purchased because if they booked up it would be one halfpenny more. They were good housekeepers and every halfpenny was important.

On Saturday, Mrs Lyons drove her back to Inverell where she again stayed at the presbytery but visited the Sisters of Mercy for recreation that evening. On Sunday 17 May she heard Mass in the sisters' part of the church and at about nine o'clock Mrs Carruthers and Maddie drove her half way to Glen Innes whilst Tom Wynne and Polly met her and drove her the rest of the way. The next day she went by train to Armidale and thence to the Ursuline convent and in the afternoon, Dean O'Connor drove her to Hillgrove where the sisters were delighted to see her. Hillgrove convent and school had been opened in 1891. The names of the sisters mentioned were Emelda Gleeson and Mechtilde McNamara. There were others but Mary did not mention their names in her report. She examined the school on two days and found 106 children on the roll. The convent was a very comfortable one consisting of seven good rooms, with a kitchen, refectory and washhouse. She declared in her report that the sisters were the

---

9. Oliver, Cathy ed. *Memories of Mary by those who knew her, Sisters of St Joseph 1925-1926* (Mulgrave, Victoria: John Garratt Publishing, 2010), 12.

most united, happy community she had seen. Mention is made in her report of the back verandah which she said was a splendid one and would have been much used in the summer. She wrote:

> I am particularly pleased with the pictures, nearly all of which are <u>poor</u> and framed in plain Oxford frames, the only gilded one being a portrait of the Dean which hangs in the reception room.[10]

Mary thought that they had better leave that one! The Dean was very kind to the sisters and Mary thought that by his cheerful fatherly kindness he had made this a particularly natural and happy community. The sisters had Mass on Sundays and Mondays and the priest stayed overnight in a room leading into the church. He had tea at the convent on Saturday and dinner on Sunday and the rest of his meals at the hotel.

She returned to Armidale, driven by the Dean, on Monday 25 May and stayed with the Ursuline Sisters. Mr Madden again did the honours and drove her to catch the train back to Uralla. At recreation that evening the sisters had some music with Sister Teresa playing the piano which she did well. At another recreation they played dominoes. The next day she took the train to Quirindi. There, that evening they had some music among themselves. The 29 May was Flora MacKillop's anniversary (the tenth) and Father Paul said Mass for her. That day Mary examined the children who were very excited about the exam. Seventy-eight of the eighty-four enrolled were examined making this a busy day.

Mary had intended to visit the Sisters of Mercy at Gunnedah but was not feeling well enough to catch a train at two o'clock in the morning, so gave up the idea. She and Sister Agnes went to Willow Tree by train to see Mrs Breton who promised to give a Ball at her own home in aid of the convent debt. On Sunday she had chats with each sister separately and gave Sisters M Rose and Cuthbert instructions concerning their begging. She remained up writing until three o'clock in the morning. Sisters Rose and Cuthbert started for Narrabri at two o'clock in the morning to do their begging to pay off the debt on the convent.

---

10. Report of Hillgrove Convent, May 1896, Mother House Archives.

On Monday 1 June she left by train for Woy Woy and shared a carriage with Mrs Breton. How did Mary pass the time? She had a long chat about the Institute, said the fifteen Mysteries of the Rosary and the Dolour rosary, and did not find the journey long!! With Sister Ann Joseph Waters and Agnes who met her at Woy Woy, she sailed part of the way to the Orphanage which they reached as darkness fell.[11] She spent the next day visiting the school, going over the place with Sister Ann Joseph and found all much improved especially the poultry yard under Sister Michael's care. She had a chat with each sister and with Agnes.

The next day she took the train to Redfern, after the boat boys had rowed her to Woy Woy and for which service she gave them a shilling to buy fishing lines. She conducted some business in the city and returned to the North Shore.

Remember that Mary was not Mother General at this time but she did almost all of the visitation of the sisters in those distant places. Mary loved making these visits because she loved the sisters and her times with them. It gave her an opportunity to see to their welfare and the circumstances in which they lived and to visit their schools and meet the priests and the parishioners.

After a few days at home she decided to visit the sisters at Penrith. This she did from Saturday, 6 June until the following Thursday. Whilst there she carried out her usual visitation programme but also drove Father Sheridan's sulky to visit some people with Sister M Antonia Wilson going part way up the mountains. On her return she had dinner and, after giving the horse a rest, drove in the pony sulky to St Marys, saw the sisters and Father Phelan and was home by dark. She returned to Sydney on the Thursday.

The sisters had been teaching at Bondi since 1894 going daily from the Providence in Cumberland Street. When land was donated by Miss O'Mara to the Bondi parish, the Franciscans who were in charge of that part of the parish, used it to build a church/school, St Anne's, on the corner of O'Brien and Simpson Streets, Bondi Beach. The first Mass in the new church was celebrated on 2 August 1896. There was a weatherboard cottage on the corner of Waverley Street (later called

---

11. Agnes was a faithful friend and assistant to the sisters and there are many references to her in Mary's diary. She was trusted with many commissions for the sisters both at the orphanage and at the North Shore convent.

Bondi Road) and Wellington Street. It stood on part of the land that had been left to the Archdiocese of Sydney by Felix McCrory, and towards the latter months of 1896 the sisters moved into this cottage. Whether they rented the cottage or were allowed the use of it is not certain. However, by 1900 the Sisters of St Joseph had purchased, from the Archdiocese, the land on which the cottage stood. The block purchased extended 4 chains (80 metres) along Waverley Street (Bondi Road) and 13 chains (260 metres) along Wellington Street and they paid £500 for it. The deed was signed by Mary MacKillop and Sisters Josephine McMullen, Patrick Barry and La Merci Mahony on 24 April 1900. The sisters continued to live in this cottage until the present two-storey convent was built and in use in 1917.[12]

Sisters Gerard Rowan and Alphonsus taught in the school in 1896. Sister Veronica Champion wrote to Mary, who was in Melbourne at the time, a letter full of complaints. One of these referred to the Bondi School which she said 'was left to Sister Gerard and Sister Alphonsus. The latter is useless in the school.'[13]

Perhaps the situation improved when the sisters moved into the convent.

St Joseph's Convent Bondi NSW. c.1906.

---

12. NSW Land and Property Management Authority, *Mary MacKillop (1842–1909) Records of a Saint*, 24.
13. Sister Veronica Champion to Mary MacKillop, 16 July 1896.

The Catholic Press had an interesting item in its issue of December 1896:

> No one would expect to find in this slowly rising suburb such a gem of a school church as the one which stands here at the foot of the hills but at some distance from the sea. The school is the prettiest I have seen. It must have been built at Nice or Cannes, and then imported to be placed among the barren hills of Bondi. Already the indefatigable Sisters of St Joseph have attracted 60 or 70 children, who are as neat, clean, and attractive as the school is.[14]

The *Freeman's Journal* in its November issue had another interesting paragraph:

> An excellent entertainment—undoubtedly the best ever presented to a Waverley audience—was given in Stratton's hall on Monday evening last, for the purpose of raising funds to furnish the residence of the above Sisters at Bondi.[15]

The article had been headed *The Sisters of St Joseph, Bondi* and gave a very full account of the items, all featuring talented adults.

When the sisters moved into their new home they enjoyed the proximity of their new school which was still a considerable distance from the convent.

In 1905 Archbishop Kelly wrote to Sister La Merci about a problem at Bondi. He asked her to intervene about this. It seems that when Sister Gabrielle Jordan, who had been teaching at the school from 1899 until 1904, was moved, the people boycotted her successor who was none other than the aristocratic Sister Francis Xavier Amsinck, one of the first to join Mary in 1866.[16] She would not have been impressed with the boycott.

Such was how Mary spent her time after the General Chapter. No wonder that Mother Bernard missed her when she left North Shore on 1 July 1896 to visit Numurkah, and the other five Josephite foundations in Victoria before going on to South Australia. When Mary arrived in Adelaide on 21 July she

---

14. *Catholic Press* Saturday, 12 December 1896, 16.
15. *Freeman's Journal,* 21 November 1896, 15.
16. Archbishop Kelly to Sister La Merci, 1905.

received a hearty welcome from [her] dear old Sisters. Came back with strangely mixed feelings— joy and sorrow and deep gratitude to our ever loving and good God.[17]

It was her first visit to Adelaide since her expulsion by Bishop Reynolds in November 1883 and Mary was able to move freely around the convents of South Australia. No new foundations were made in New South Wales during 1897 but Mary kept in constant contact with Mother Bernard whilst she was absent. When she had finished her work in Adelaide she went to Melbourne where she embarked for New Zealand in October 1897. Mother Bernard came on board the boat that would take Mary and some sisters to New Zealand. Neither Mary nor Mother Bernard realised then that this was to be their final farewell.

From Temuka, New Zealand, Mary wrote to her brother, Father Donald, a letter in which she opened her heart and revealed the sufferings she had undergone in the past. She wrote:

> Excepting that I lost my temper with MG on one particular occasion, which I shall ever regret for I forgot what I owed to her in her position, and that I could not honestly feel that she was either true or just, I really did resist the temptations against submission and my vocation, though they were awful while they lasted.

As an explanation she revealed that

> often when smarting under insults and misrepresentations which I longed to resent, I would have to go and do the 'dirty work', as many call it, simply because I could not resist God's pleading voice or look. Ah, God was good to me. I see it all now more plainly than ever.[18]

Throughout the previous years this had been the pattern and had been the cause of tension between the two. Whilst Mary was in New Zealand, Mother Bernard found it very difficult to operate without her and wrote on 25 March 1898:

---

17. Mary MacKillop's Diary, 21 July 1896.
18. Mary MacKillop to Donald MacKillop, 29 December 1897.

> I wish you were able to come home, surely things can get on without you now. You could pay a visit again next year. It is not long to go over.[19]

Mary did come home but not under the circumstances that Mother Bernard expected. She would pay another visit to New Zealand but not the next year. Many momentous events occurred before Mary's next visit to the New Zealand sisters for Christmas 1900.

---

19. Mother Bernard to Mary MacKillop, 20 March 1898.

Chapter Eleven
Death and a New Beginning 1898–1899

Mother Bernard died suddenly in August 1898 and, as Assistant General, Mary had to hasten back from Auckland to pick up the reins of government of the Congregation. Her first task was to arrange Mother Bernard's funeral and then to begin making preparations for the General Chapter for the election of a new Mother General as the Constitutions prescribed. This time Cardinal Moran acceded to all, shocked by the sudden death of Mother Bernard. The Decree of 25 July 1888 had confirmed Mother Bernard as Mother General for a further ten years, that is, until 25 July 1898. By obtaining a special rescript from Rome Cardinal Moran had confirmed her in this position until the Chapter of 1902. On 3 August 1898 just eight days after the expiry of the ten year period, Mother Bernard was dead! He said that he would not interfere again.[1]

Although Mary was busy with letter writing in preparation for the Chapter, she hurried to Glen Innes on 14 August where her beloved Sister Josephine McMullen was very ill. Mary brought her back to Sydney where she underwent an operation in September.

During August Mary was in contact with Sister Aloysius Lenihan at Dapto where the school and convent were to be moved from West Dapto, because the new railway had by-passed West Dapto. Sister Aloysius had found a piece of land suitable for a convent and school on a site not far from the railway.

Mary devoted the month of October to preparations for the forthcoming Chapter which was held 10-11 January 1899 with forty sisters

---

1. It was Cardinal Moran who was instrumental in prolonging Mother Bernard's time in office. Rescripts from Rome came only in response to written requests.

present. Mary was re-elected and she had as her councillors four very efficient and experienced sisters, namely Sisters Josephine McMullen, La Merci Mahony, Patrick Barry and Patricia Campbell.

After the Chapter Mary set out to visit every convent and school in the Congregation. This was a tremendous undertaking and over the next three years, she travelled many thousands of miles in all kinds of conveyances and in every kind of weather. She did not spare herself in this extraordinary effort.

In between dealing with the many business matters of the growing Congregation, Mary visited the sisters in the scattered parts of New South Wales. On Saturday, 4 March 1899 she went to Kiama with Sister Dympna. While there she met with Father Barlow, well-known to her as her meetings with him at various places have been mentioned in these pages. She examined the school of thirty-nine pupils on two days. She saw that the school room required lining on the inside and painting on the outside. No doubt she informed Father Barlow about the state of the school and suggested that he remedy the situation. She noted in her report that the people were not generous and Sisters Justina Lupton and Finbar Foley found it hard to make ends meet, as the average weekly school fees were only six shillings and eight pence.

While there she managed to fit in a visit to MacKillop relations and then she and Sister Justina went to Berry where she interviewed the sisters and examined the school, even though only a few children were present. She had a pleasant evening with the Berry sisters and returned to Kiama the next morning. She went back to Berry by the night train arriving at ten–thirty, evidently so that she could meet Father Greening. She finished examining the Berry school and returned on the train, dropping Sister Justina off at Kiama and meeting up with Sister Dympna who went with her to Albion Park where she met with Father Hayden.

On Thursday she interviewed each sister and the next day examined the school and gave the sisters an instruction on various matters relating to their life as sisters. Sister Aloysius then drove her to West Dapto where on the Friday she examined the school, gave an instruction to the sisters and interviewed each one privately. She spent a happy day there and on the next day, 11 March, she and Sister Aloysius started for Sydney. At Bulli, Sister Francis Xavier met her at the station and they spent a few minutes in conversation. This was something that often happened in those days as the trains meandered from place to place staying at each station for long enough to make it worthwhile for the sisters to trek there.

Two weeks of business followed for Mary, taking her in and around the city, the Providence and North Shore and then she was on the steamer heading for Eden, where she landed on Sunday 26 March and was met by Sisters Pierre O'Shannessy and Elizabeth. She stayed there until 18 April with this community which was made up of Sisters M. Pierre, Zita and Elizabeth. Their convent, a two-storey wooden building, overlooked the ocean. The church, a wooden one, was also used as a school. The priest said Sunday Mass in Eden once a month and on three week days each month.

Mary went from Eden to Bombala on Easter Sunday, being driven by Mr McCabe as far as Lochiel, where she stayed for two nights with the family. Next day Mr McCabe drove her up the Big Jack Mountain to Bombala. He had trouble getting a horse and she noted in her diary that it was a poor half-starved thing. Evidently it managed to haul the sulky up the mountain because she arrived safely. Driver and horse made the return journey to Lochiel after they had something to eat. No doubt Mary saw to it that the horse had a substantial feed and a friendly pat on the head.

Lochiel NSW. 2014. Once the home of the McCabe family where Mary spent two nights at Eastertime 1899. Photo provided by Bernadette O'Sullivan rsj. Used with permission.

Back in May 1889, the Catholics of Bombala saw that the sisters required a new convent and at a meeting decided that it could be erected on the site of the existing structure in Maharatta Street at a cost of £1,000.² Completed by May 1891 this convent was where Mary visited from 4–11 April. She found that the school building, the old slab hotel, was in a very unsatisfactory state. When the parish priest, Father Norris, called on her she had a long chat with him over school matters. When he said Mass in the convent the next day, she again spoke about making some improvements to the school. Next time Father Norris came he had good news for her. He drove her to see the church which was quite a distance from the convent. On the following Saturday she was pleased to see that the carpenters were at work in the school. All the time Mary was at Bombala it was very wet and when there was a poor attendance at the school on Monday, she dismissed the children and gave the two fifth class girls some special lessons in the music room in the afternoon. Mary noted in her diary that she had bought a box of dominoes for the sisters so that they now had a new occupation during their recreation time.

Mary reported that the community, a happy one, consisted of Sisters Stephanie Brady who had arrived there in 1890, Agatha Doherty who had entered in Brisbane during Mary's time there in 1879 and had been in Bombala since 1892, Aiden Madden and Martina Bunfield. The convent which was owned by the parish was very comfortable. The two pianos belonged to the sisters. Mass was said in the Oratory once a week.

Next she travelled by coach to Cooma where she visited the Brigidine Sisters and then caught the train for Bungendore where she arrived at ten-thirty. It was a dark wet night but Sisters Clare George and Maria Joseph Hearney were there with horse and sulky to meet her. This visit lasted from 11–17 April. The following day she visited the priests, Fathers Birch and Grace. They asked for sisters for Captains Flat so the next day Father Grace drove her to this booming mining town which, at its peak in the 1890s boasted six general stores and five hotels.³

---

2. *Australian Town and Country Journal*, 25 May 1889, 14.
3. Susan Pryke, *Boom to Bust and Back Again*, Captains Flat, NSW: Residents and Ratepayers Association, 1983, 11.

By 1898 the town had three doctors, two dentists, a chemist, a watchmaker and jeweller, three hairdressers, a tailor, a blacksmith, and an insurance agent. There were several auctioneers in the town, assorted billiard halls, a cordial factory, a medical hall, a School of Arts, a printing office, and a newspaper.[4]

The original Roman Catholic Chapel (no longer standing) had been completed in June 1890. On the way Mary and Father Grace called at *The Briars*, the home of Mr and Mrs Shanahan where they dined with the family. A further stop was made at the home of the Osbornes where they had to get a fresh horse before going on to Captains Flat. Finally, after a drive of thirty-two miles, they reached their destination where Father Grace showed Mary the church and the cottage he had proposed as a convent. At Mrs Cooper's Hotel where they stayed the night, a number of the wives met them. The next day some of the men came after breakfast and they decided to rent the cottage which the priest would use until the sisters came. On the return journey they called at the Osborne's for the pony and then on to Mrs Shanahan's. She drove Mary back to the convent after she had visited old Mrs Sheehan and family, Mrs Seery and Mrs Walsh and daughters.[5] The indefatigable Mary was always diligent in visiting friends she had made on her previous journeys and making new ones. Nobody was neglected.

Captains Flat NSW. 2014. Photo taken from the Lookout overlooking the town. Photo provided by Bernadette O'Sullivan rsj. Used with permission.

---

4. Pryke, *Boom to Bust and Back Again*, 1983, 13.
5. Mary MacKillop's Diary, 1899.

In her report Mary stated that the convent at Bungendore was a comfortable eight-roomed two-storey house that was parish property. It had a nice oratory on the upper floor that was badly in need of a coat of paint. There were four sisters in this happy community: Sisters Mary Clare, Maria Joseph, Anne and a Postulant.

The next day after Mass Mary received Queenie McGrath and Katie Colls as postulants. She visited their parents the following day. Queenie's older sister had entered the sisters about 1888 and was known in religion as Sister Celsus.[6] Katie Colls was the fourth daughter of Mr and Mrs Neil Colls. That night, Mary, accompanied by the two postulants (and a crate of live turkeys), travelled by train to Sydney. She was unable to visit Araluen this time and had to arrange for her letters to be sent to her at Bungendore. Obviously, she had intended to visit Araluen but the business of Captains Flat precluded this, to the disappointment of that community.

Mary wasted no time when she got back to Sydney and over the next few months, she and the council decided to open the school and convent at Captains Flat. On 19 June 1899, Mary was able to inform Father Grace:

> We have fixed on two very excellent and energetic Sisters for Captains Flat and these will be ready to start about the middle of July.[7]

Mary was very firm about the conditions attached to this foundation and stated that before the sisters left for Captains Flat furniture to the value of sixty pounds should be provided. If Father sent a cheque for that amount the furniture could be purchased in Sydney and she would have it sent by steamer to Nelligan and then by carrier to Captains Flat. The lady from the hotel at Captains Flat had told her that it was cheaper to send goods by steamer than by rail.

She went on further to ask him to inform the committee that if they wanted a good school, they must pay for it and provide decent furniture for the convent and school. She wrote:

---

6. Queenie McGrath left the Congregation at a later date. Sister Celsus, her sister, died in 1908.
7. Mary MacKillop to Father Grace, 19 June 1899.

They are getting good Sisters who, with one concert, will do wonders in paying for what is laid out in furnishing. Please do not buy any of the furniture up there. The house is so small that to manage at all we must select furniture that will suit us for it.[8]

The desks were to be made on a plan approved by the sister in charge of the school. Mary added that she hoped to accompany them but as will be seen, she did not manage to do this. Finally, she told Father that the sisters would provide the piano.

An after note informed him that if the sisters could get the furniture for less than sixty pounds she would return the balance to help pay the freight. Mary had learnt many a lesson in the past about new foundations where promises were made but not carried out, thus forcing the sisters to suffer privations.

From Mary's diary some snippets of information tell us that the cheque was forthcoming as she was able to buy a Tabernacle for Captains Flat and that she had previously paid a deposit on a piano. She also bought books and blinds. No doubt other purchases were made by some of her assistants. This was a good example of Mary's planning for new openings.

On the feast of the Patronage of St Joseph, 23 April, eight novices received the habit from Bishop Higgins. When she received word that an apprentice had died at the orphanage, Mary left the ceremony and, taking Sister Luigi Meade, arrived there to find the sisters in great distress. No priest was available to conduct the burial, so the sisters performed the ceremony for the boy. No doubt Mary and the sisters prayed fervently for the child. She returned to Sydney on Friday, 28 April, and the following day visited Rookwood (Lidcombe), Bankstown and the Providence before departing for Bulli.

At Bulli she had the usual round of conferences with the sisters and gave an instruction. The next day she went by train to Dapto. The sisters did not meet her and she had to walk from the station to the convent at West Dapto, a considerable distance. Nevertheless she had a truly happy night there. The next day Sister Aloysius drove her to see the site for the new convent and later to the train.

---

8. Mary MacKillop to Father Grace, 19 June 1899.

Back in Sydney she had to attend to business about some new buildings at the Orphanage and some land at Glen Innes. She went to the Orphanage on Saturday, 27 May, taking two orphans with her.

On Monday she returned to Sydney. Two days later she set out for Melbourne with Sister Justine. After stopping off at Numurkah they went on to Melbourne on the evening train the next day. Two weeks later she returned to Sydney.

In the space of a few days after her return she and Sister Aloysius had seen Mr Armstrong about the Dapto deeds and bought books. After six o'clock Mass the next day, she and Sister Aloysius visited the Kincumber Orphanage and returned the same day, very tired! On the 21 June she paid an overnight visit to Lithgow. At the same time, she was negotiating with Bishop Duhig for a foundation for the Rockhampton diocese.

On Sunday 2 July, several sisters were received and others were professed at Mount Street, North Sydney. No visitors were invited and, as the ceremonies were very long, no sermon was preached. Sister Virgilius O'Shea, was professed on her death bed. She died on 23 August.

On one of her many trips into the city with Sister La Merci, Mary purchased a typewriter for which she paid twenty-four pounds ten shillings. This was a large amount but Mary could see the advantage such an instrument would be for Sister La Merci who learnt to use it as did others, saving time and, unknown to her then, she would use it herself in later years.

On 22 July 1899 she started for Armidale, accompanied as far as Redfern station by two Irish-born sisters, Sister Jerome Cahill, aged thirty-nine years and Sister Raymond Elliot, aged twenty-eight years. These two were the foundation community for Captains Flat. Their fares were paid as far as Bungendore and they were given money for extras. These were the two excellent and energetic sisters, Mary had chosen to take up residence in the small cottage, hopefully, already furnished.

Sister Jerome had lived at Waimate in the South Island of New Zealand and, according to Mary's letter to Sister Raymond Smyth, wanted to leave there. The priest, Father Regnault sm, was not happy about this and Mary had to write to him a strong letter in which she let him know that it was for the sake of Sister Jerome's vocation that she was recalling her to Sydney. She wrote:

> I appeal to yourself as a Religious and a guide of souls—would I have been justified in insisting upon a subject's remaining when she was unhappy and in daily danger of sinning against her vow of obedience.[9]

Sister Jerome came to Sydney before 20 June 1899 and was soon on her way to Captains Flat.

Mary arrived at Quirindi at about seven o'clock. She visited with the sisters the next day and left the following morning on the two-thirty morning train for Uralla. Sisters Casimir and Donatus saw her off and she reached Uralla in time for Mass. She found the sisters well and happy, visited the school, and had recreation with them in the dormitory as she was to start for Glen Innes by the early morning train. There she was met by Sisters Blandina and Anthony Melville. Here she interviewed each sister and on 25 July 1899 wrote a circular letter to all members of the Congregation. The next day she took the morning train to Tenterfield. As was her custom, she visited the children in the school, interviewed the sisters, received visitors, and met with the priest. The people were generous and she collected fowls and eggs for the orphanage at Kincumber. Knowing that she had many places to visit, Mary probably arranged for the fowls and eggs to be sent on to Kincumber. It would never do for her to be seen travelling with a crate of fowls and boxes of eggs! That evening she caught the train for Glen Innes. From there Sisters Blandina and Julia saw her off on the train for Armidale.

When Mary reached the Ursuline sisters' convent at Armidale it was late and it was midnight when she retired to bed. The next day the Bishop said Mass at the convent and she had an interview with him before Father O'Sullivan drove her to Hillgrove where she arrived at one-thirty in the afternoon. She was ill on Saturday night—no wonder!

Sunday Mass was at 11 o'clock. Before that she interviewed each sister and gave them an instruction. Sister Ambrosine was one of the sisters mentioned. Father O'Sullivan drove Mary halfway to Armidale and the Dean drove her the rest of the way.

She left by the night train for Quirindi and arrived there at half past three the following morning. That day she saw the sisters and the children, gave lollies and a play to the latter and started for Gosford

---

9. Mary MacKillop to Father Regnault SM, 20 May 1899.

by train. She had a cold wet drive to the orphanage where she arrived late that evening. She did not rise early the next day as she had a heavy cold. Agnes was very pleased with the fowls and eggs and Mary was pleased to know that they had arrived safely.

Back at North Shore Mary immediately got down to business. On Friday she received word that Sister Veronica Champion was gravely ill at Villa Maria. She died on Sunday 6 August. During this time, Mary attended to the affairs of the new building being erected at the orphanage, Kincumber. She paid accounts, saw solicitors and others concerned with the building. With the death of Sister Veronica she had to sort out hers and Mother Bernard's papers, a task completed on 19 August.[10]

On 3 September she caught the train to Melbourne stayed there for five days then travelled to Adelaide and visited the sisters there for about five weeks before she returned to Melbourne via Bacchus Marsh where she arrived on Friday 13 October. The end result of all this work brought on an illness that meant that she was unable to return to Sydney until the end of October.

In November she spent time at Kincumber orphanage and when she returned to Sydney she bought Christmas toys for the children. In her circular of 7 December she asked prayers that 'money will come in for the new orphanage building'.[11]

Mary's first full year as Mother General since her re-election was one of many journeys undertaken as if she was filled with an urgency to give herself completely to her sisters, their wellbeing and the needs of the church and world.

---

10. Sister Veronica Champion had been on the General Council with the title Procuratrix General (Bursar) from 1889 until the Chapter of 1899 so had only had a short time of retirement before she died.
11. Mary MacKillop to the sisters, 7 December 1899.

Chapter Twelve
More Foundations in 1900 and 1901

Meanwhile, the Candelo foundation went ahead. On 26 December 1899 Father T Hartnett wrote to Cardinal Moran the following:

> I beg to state that the Candelo convent will be fit for occupation next week. It is hoped you will come and formally open it, and that the Sisters will start school there on the fifteenth of January.[1]

The *Freeman's Journal*, 3 March 1900 gave the information:

> A few weeks ago the Mother General and three Sisters of the Order of St Joseph arrived in Candelo for the purpose of installing the incoming community [the three Sisters] in the new convent recently erected for the Order at a cost of £900. A short time ago the commanding situation upon which the building is erected was open common ground; today it lends a picturesque appearance to the place having on it a substantial building of architectural beauty . . . and today we have a new institution with an increasing attendance of 80 pupils some of whom are boarding, all healthy, happy and contented for the benign influence of these good Sisters is already apparent.[2]

Mary could possibly have taken the sisters to Candelo although she was in Numurkah on 12 January. If it was not Mary it was either Sister La Merci Mahony, her Assistant, or one of the other Councillors.

---

1. Rev T Hartnett to Cardinal Moran, 28 December 1899.
2. *Freeman's Journal*, 3 March 1900, 16.

St Joseph's Convent Candelo NSW. c.1906.

Mary did not forget the Candelo sisters and their school and she appealed to all the sisters for help for a bazaar that the sisters were involved in. She was pleased with their response and, in a circular, wrote

> And now, dearest Sisters, let me thank you for the generous manner in which you have responded to my call for help for the Candelo Bazaar. Thanks to your generosity (S. Australia, Victoria and Armidale having assisted), I have been able to send sufficient to furnish a stall well. In this we are helping to have things made much easier for our Sisters there and helping the cause of our school.[3]

Nothing escaped Mary's notice and she had the ability to call forth the practical generosity of all the sisters to help a new foundation, and, thus, another means of keeping the sisters united.

Candelo was the centre of a rich dairying district and there were some very good Catholic families in the area. As happened in many other instances, a grand entertainment was provided by the children on Wednesday 5 September 1900. There were then seventy children enrolled and they entertained a very appreciative audience. This was a fundraiser to help with the building costs.[4] Concerts became an

---

3. Mary MacKillop to the sisters, 24 February 1900.
4. *Southern Star,* 8 September 1900, 2.

Candelo Catholic School, Candelo NSW. 1901. Mother Mary MacKillop in top row, far right.
Photo provided by Jim Alcock. Used with permission.

annual event and the one that was held on 15 December 1903 surpassed all others.[5]

Mary was at the opening of the Numurkah convent on 12 January 1900. On 11 February she wrote thanking the sisters for their help with the Candelo Bazaar so as 'to have things much easier for our sisters there, and helping the cause of our schools'.[6]

The early part of 1900 was taken up with preparations for the opening of the new building at Kincumber. Mary wrote to her good friend Sister Ethelburg Job, telling her that

> the new wing at the Orphanage is an imposing building—will be formally opened DV in Easter week.[7] The Cardinal says we must make a big affair of it, special trains, private steam yachts, etc etc to be employed, and as His Eminence says 'plenty money to be taken.' I hope so in any case.[8]

---

5. *Freeman's Journal*, 2 January 1904, 36.
6. Mary MacKillop to the sisters, 29 Feb 1900.
7. DV meaning Deo Volente, God Willing.
8. Mary MacKillop to Sister Ethelburg Job, 5 March 1900.

The Cardinal blessed and opened the extension on 17 April 1900. A report of the event in the *Sydney Morning Herald* mentioned that 'Fr Paul of Quirindi presented the institution with 100 merino sheep'. What a wonderful gift the sheep were and one wonders if Mary had been canvassing among her sisters and their priests for donations for the new building which consisted of 'a concert hall, eighty feet by fifty feet, and a dormitory adjoining of the same dimensions'.[9] On 11 August 1900 the following report appeared in *The Catholic Press*:

> It was in the year 1887 that the Sisters began to find their house in Cumberland Street all too small for the work in which they were engaged. They thought it would be a splendid thing if they could get some farm in the country for the orphan boys under their care, where they would be able to train them advantageously and under healthier conditions. It would mean too, more room in the Providence for the many applicants that daily besieged them. No sooner was His Eminence the Cardinal apprised of their ambition than he put at their disposal the four-roomed cottage at Kincumber which had been the priests' residence. It was an ideal spot for the work; the frontage was on the beautiful Brisbane Water, the back fence halted at the edge of virgin bush; the 13 acres which comprised the property consisted of good agricultural and arable land and when the Sisters first looked over their little property their ears caught the sounds of the future, and they could hear the lowing of milking cows, the clucking of hens, and the noise of threshers in the barns, and could also see little orphan lads growing up in the sunshine and fresh air into tanned and hardy youth full of farmers' and settlers' craft, the type that Australia wants so badly.
>
> They set to work at once to convert the cottage to their needs and assisted by Father Madden the priest in charge of the district who was a good friend to the orphans, and a cheering friend to the Sisters, they soon had their work under way and 22 boys translated from the Providence to this bright new home under the charge of three Sisters.
>
> The cottage expanded in time, the boundary fence grew more embracing and the little orphans increased in numbers, whilst

---

9. *Sydney Morning Herald*, 27 April 1900, 3.

just as the Sisters had dreamed it cows lowed and poultry clucked and grain grew ripe for the threshers. Kincumber rose to all occasions and His Eminence had no cause to regret his practical encouragement. From 1887 to 1892 the pretty farm received 101 orphans, and of them 31 were apprenticed when old enough and useful enough to begin life; and when His Eminence the Cardinal, his Grace Archbishop Carr [of Melbourne] and his Lordship Dr Corbett (Bishop of Sale) paid the institution a visit in the latter year they found 70 orphans being educated and trained. For maintenance Kincumber was absolutely dependant on the Providence, and on its behalf four Sisters went forth to collect every day. It was about this period that the late Dr Sheridan began to manifest an interest in the institution and from then until the day of his death Kincumber was never without his support.

The new schoolroom and dormitories that were recently erected at Kincumber cost £1,072, on which remains a debt of £400.[10]

This was obviously another appeal for financial assistance.

Buildings went up in a number of places and when Mary wrote to the sisters on 6 March 1900 she hoped that 'by mid-winter we shall have our Free School erected'.[11] A Free School was one established for the poor children of the area. School fees were not charged.

This school was built at North Sydney on the site of a wooden building that was used as a free school (1891–1899) for training teachers. It was demolished and a brick school room built on the site, a corner of the Mount Street property and what was then Alma Lane below the Alma Terrace houses.[12] A stone set high up on the front of the building can still be seen today and reads *St Joseph's School 1900*. The 1896 General Chapter had turned its attention to the classification of the newly-professed sisters before sending them out as teachers. The Chapter appointed Sisters Baptista Molloy and La Merci Mahony to examine the sisters in different branches of secular subjects. This examination helped them classify these teachers before appointments

---

10. *Catholic Press*, 11 August 1900, 12.
11. Mary MacKillop to the sisters, 6 March 1900.
12. Kathleen Burford, 'Buildings of St Joseph's Convent Mount Street North Sydney', unpublished manuscript.

were made. This was the commencement of the St Joseph's Teacher Training School which later became the Catholic Teachers' College open to lay women in 1958 and now [2017]a part of the Australian Catholic University.

In May 1900, Mary went twice to Dapto where a new convent was blessed and opened on 9 May. She had helped the sisters prepare the convent for the opening over which Cardinal Moran presided.

Opening Day at St Joseph's Convent Dapto NSW. 9 May 1900. Cardinal Moran, in top hat, is seated in the foreground.

St Joseph's Convent Dapto NSW. c.1901. Sisters left to right: Wilfrid Connell, Aloysius Lenihan, Columbanus Considine and Marcellinus Mulheron.

From there she proceeded to Helensburgh where Sisters Emilian Dempsey, Louis Mary Daly and a postulant opened the school on 14 May 1900. On that first day they enrolled fifty-six pupils and Mary wrote to Sister Benedict at the orphanage that the same number of children were enrolled at the new opening at Drummoyne. She also asked Sister Benedict to see Mr Thompson and thank him for procuring a bull for the farm and also a nice cow that she wanted to pay for.[13] What a contrast in this letter where she spoke of the school enrolments at the new schools and then remembered the bull and the cow at Kincumber. Even such mundane matters as the purchase of farm animals did not escape Mary's attention. And what had happened to the 100 merino sheep from Quirindi?

St Joseph's Convent Helensburgh NSW. c.1906.

The blessing of additions to Drummoyne parish church in 1929 was reported in an article in the *Freeman's Journal*.[14] It quoted Bishop Sheehan who recalled that the church had served as a schoolhouse on week days, taught by two ladies until the Sisters of the Good Samaritan took over.[15] They gave place to the Sisters of St Joseph who had purchased their own convent in 5 Plunket Street in 1900. It was an old

---

13. Mary MacKillop to Sister Benedict, Kincumber, 22 May 1900.
14. *Freeman's Journal*, 11 April 1929, 17.
15. Bishop Sheehan was coadjutor to Archbishop Kelly of Sydney from 1922 until July 1937 when he resigned and returned to Ireland.

two-storey weatherboard house at a long distance from the church-school. This convent was replaced in 1905 by the purchase of another house which was later improved and extended.[16]

St Joseph's Convent Drummoyne NSW. c.1906.

Mary followed the progress of the Drummoyne school in her usual way and she was pleased to learn that on 1 November the sisters organised the first annual school picnic for 100 children. This took place at Rodd Island in Iron Cove. The *Freeman's Journal* reported that 'the homeward journey started at 5.30 after spending a jolly good day's outing.'[17]

That year 1900 caused other headaches for Mary as the bubonic plague broke out in The Rocks where the Providence and St Michael's Marist Church were located. The Government resumed land in the area and the Marists agreed that St Michael's would be sold to the Government. On 19 March 1901 the Sisters of St Joseph also accepted remuneration for the Providence Building of three floors and a basement. They used the money received to pay for a building they had already purchased on the Pacific Highway Lane Cove. Later 'the Josephite Providence served as the Public works department cement testing branch in 1902–1903 and became afterwards the premises of the State Labour bureau.'[18] An interesting paragraph in the *Catholic Press* asked that

---

16. Burford, *Unfurrowed Fields*, 82.
17. *Freeman's Journal*, 17 November 1900, 22.
18. Peter McMurrich, *The Harmonising Influence of Religion: St Patrick's Church Hill, 1840 to the Present*, (Sydney: Patrick Books, 2011), 45.

All correspondence hitherto addressed there [the Providence] may now be sent to St Joseph's Convent North Sydney. Telephone No. 123.[19]

Eventually the Providence was demolished as was St Michael's Church which had been the scene of many Receptions and Professions of sisters. It was at St Michael's that Flora MacKillop's Requiem took place back in 1886. When the Providence closed, the Sisters of Mercy took charge of the former Josephite school in St Bridget's Church in Kent Street. They began teaching there at the end of January 1901.

In August 1900 Mary and the sisters purchased 'Gladstone House' a property of ten acres overlooking the Lane Cove River. This became a residence for the orphan girls from the Providence in Cumberland Street. The sisters and thirty-seven young girls moved in on 19 March 1901.[20] Sister Agnes Smith was appointed Superior. Mary, busy as usual, was on hand to assist with the transfer. The Home was formally blessed and opened by Cardinal Moran on 17 November of that same year. Mary was a proud attendee at this event and happy that the sisters and girls had been removed from the Rocks area and were now able to enjoy the healthy surroundings of their new home.

St Joseph's Girls' Home Lane Cove NSW. Undated.

---

19. *Catholic Press*, 11 May 1901, 13.
20. Burford, *Unfurrowed Fields*, 81.

It was in August 1900 that Mary received a letter from Sister Gonzaga Delaney, the Sister Guardian of the small group of diocesan Sisters at Bungaree in Victoria. They had been founded from Perthville in 1891. For the first time they had read of the Decree of 1888 allowing any diocesan Sister to join the Sisters of St Joseph of the Sacred Heart at North Sydney. They were unhappy at Bungaree and they asked if Mary would receive them. Mary assured them that she would but their Bishop, Bishop Moore of Ballarat, would not give permission. Mary was in Melbourne at this time so visited these sisters at Bungaree for two nights and was impressed with their spirit. She was unable to see Bishop Moore on this occasion but with Cardinal Moran's agreement and the consent of her Council to accept the sisters, she paid a further visit to them but even then the bishop would not see her. At last, on yet another visit towards the end of October, she met him and he finally agreed to allow the sisters to leave.[21]

The novices and postulants, who did not need the bishop's permission to go to North Sydney, had already left for Melbourne where they were joined by Sister Colette and another postulant and together they all set off by steamer for Sydney. Mary waited until the last of the Bungaree sisters arrived in Melbourne and she joined them for the train trip to Sydney on 6 November 1900.[22] The sisters who had decided to amalgamate with the centrally governed Congregation based in North Sydney, then renewed their vows according to the Constitutions of the Sisters of St Joseph of the Sacred Heart. Mary's heart rejoiced at this amalgamation of the Victorian sisters from Bungaree.

True to her decision to visit all the convents of the order as soon as possible after the 1899 Chapter, Mary was in New Zealand from 2 December 1900 until 11 February 1901. Then, wasting no time, she left for Melbourne on 29 April 1901, again visited the sisters before travelling by express to Adelaide staying there from 10-20 May. She returned to Melbourne after breaking her journey at Bacchus Marsh. After concluding many business affairs in Melbourne she returned to Sydney and arrived on 27 June. The advent of the railway in the previous century meant quicker travel between Sydney, Melbourne and

---

21. Marie Crowley, *Except in Obedience: The Diocesan Sisters of St Joseph in Victoria* (Sydney: Trustees of the Sisters of St Joseph of the Sacred Heart, 2013), 65–67.
22. Crowley, *Except in Obedience*, 69.

Adelaide. She no longer had to depend on the old Cobb & Co coaches or the coastal steamers as of yore.[23]

On 5 July she made a quick visit to Quirindi, this time taking a postulant with her and Sister Evangelista Carr for Tenterfield. Having accompanied the sisters there she returned to the North Shore on 8 July taking Sister Marcella back with her. Presumably, there was some need for a change at Tenterfield though Mary, in her diary, did not go into detail. Mary did not spare herself where the welfare of the sisters was concerned and she thought nothing of the distances she had to traverse and the inconveniences incurred. From her diary we learn that on her return from the quick trip to Quirindi she had to spend the day in bed on the feast of Our Lady of Mount Carmel, 16 July, but was happy to learn that the Mount Street School, inspected that day by Father Whyte, received a good report.[24]

Nothing escaped her attention, neither school reports, nor anything to do with the sisters and their schools. She knew that the unity of the sisters would be ensured by her constancy in visitation, and when she could not visit, by her circular letters and her very personal letters that flowed from her busy pen to individual sisters. Few, if any, letters from the sisters remained unanswered. If she was unable to write to a sister she sent a message to her by another sister.

She wrote to Sister Raymond Smyth that day and mentioned the two invalids, Sisters M Bede and Francis who were suffering from tuberculosis. She wrote:

> We have promised the Doctors that they are the last of the consumptive patients we will keep in this house. The Doctors insist on this for the sake of the young ones here, and they are right. We are going to keep Dr Sheridan's cottage . . . for the purpose. It is not too far from the house here and the invalids can exercise in the garden and attend Mass in the Oratory when well enough.[25]

Sister Bede Gunn died on 22 September 1901 and Sister Francis Goodyer died on 31 July 1901.

The following year a cottage was acquired at Katoomba and from then on the consumptive patients were transferred there.

---

23. The railway line from Sydney to Melbourne opened in 1883 and that between Melbourne and Adelaide in 1887.
24. Mary MacKillop's Diary, 1901.
25. Mary MacKillop to Sister Raymond Smyth, 16 July 1901.

Chapter Thirteen
Mary Mackillop's Three Week Visitation of the South East of NSW 1901

Mary's diary for 1901 tells a wonderful tale of her visitation of the convents in the south-east of New South Wales, the second time she visited this area after her re-election in 1899.[1] Mary did not spare herself as she followed a gruelling schedule she had set for herself. It seemed that she felt an urgency that was driving her on in her quest for the unity of the sisters in their communities and in the congregation as a whole. As well as seeing to the well-being of the sisters she sought and often insisted that improvements be carried out in their often ramshackle schools. The story is worth telling in its entirety.

So it was that Mary journeyed from Sydney on Wednesday, 24 July 1901 to visit the convents which were still located in the Archdiocese of Sydney. This part of the Archdiocese was not incorporated into the Goulburn Diocese until 1917. There were Josephite communities at Bungendore, Captains Flat, Araluen, Candelo, Eden and Bombala. At each place Mary examined the schools, had conferences with each sister in the community, gave instructions to the sisters, visited parishioners, was visited by parishioners and also visited and was visited by the priests in each parish. She travelled by steamer, cab, train, horse-drawn coach as well as by horse and buggy when there were no coach routes. She kept a meticulous account of money spent and money received, of letters received and letters answered. She also mentioned people who gave her donations in kind.

Setting out from Sydney accompanied by Sister Ann Joseph and May Murray, she boarded the train for Bungendore at Redfern. Sisters Columba and M Joseph were on the Mittagong station to catch

---

1. Mary MacKillop's Diary, 1901

a quick word with her. When they reached Bungendore Sisters Clare and Raphael and Father O'Driscoll were on the platform to meet them. Father had his horse and buggy and drove them to the convent. Hopefully, it was warm after the cold train trip.

In the morning Mary wrote letters, and then spent the afternoon examining the school and surprising the children with boiled lollies and a holiday for the next day. She did this so that she could spend time with the sisters and meet with the priests—Fathers O'Driscoll, Collander and Birch. On the Saturday Father O'Driscoll drove her to Captains Flat, distant about twenty-seven miles, where the sisters had opened a school just two years previously. She was anxious to see how they were progressing. It was a bitterly cold day but Mary enjoyed the drive, visiting her old acquaintances, Mrs Shanahan and Mrs Walsh on the way.

At Captains Flat it snowed the next day, Sunday, and, as it was still snowing heavily on Monday the school was closed. She had interviews with each sister and managed to visit parishioners in the afternoon. She enquired into school and money matters before Father O'Driscoll returned to Bungendore and a Mr Roache called to make arrangements about her journey to Araluen the next day. The school was open and so she spent time with the children, distributed lollies and gave them extra play. She had bought lollies and calico and one wonders what on earth the calico was for?[2] At about eleven o'clock Mr Roache called for her and drove her to Araluen, a distance of twenty-six miles. The way was over rough, narrow roads climbing the high mountain range and then descending into the beautiful Araluen valley. This journey took four and a half hours and she arrived at three-thirty that afternoon.

The sisters gave her a great welcome because she had been unable to visit them on her 1899 visitation. The fact that she was not able to rise for Mass the next morning tells its own tale! However, the priest, Father Baugh came to see her and she was well enough to spend time in the school with the children to whom she gave lollies and a half holiday which enabled her to meet with the sisters as was her custom. Father Baugh noticed how she travelled in the cold and gave her a rug. The next day he said Mass in the oratory after which she again saw the children in the school.

---

2. The sisters used unbleached calico to make their undergarments and bed sheets.

The next stage of her journey was by coach and Sister Finbar Foley gave her £2 toward her fare. The coach that took her for an overnight stay at Moruya, a distance of forty miles, travelled over high mountain roads and it was seven o'clock before she arrived at the convent of the Sisters of the Good Samaritan where Sister Justine and her community received her kindly. Even at that late hour Mary received a visit from a Mrs Teare. The evening was tinged with sadness as a telegram that announced the death of Sister Mary Frances Goodyer awaited her.

It is hoped that Mary had an early night because she had to be ready to catch the coach at half past four the next morning for the long trip to Bega. She set out in bitterly cold weather, freezing all the way. The horses were changed at Bodalla and again at Tilba where Mary had a breakfast of coffee and bread and butter and when the coach reached Cobargo she had dinner. She reached Bega at six-thirty. The journey of eighty-four miles had taken fourteen hours. Mary spent the night with the Sisters of Charity who received her very kindly. She organised for the coach to call for her at six o'clock the next morning to take her to Candelo but it failed to arrive.

Father Comaskey borrowed Father Barnett's good buggy and pair—how delightful for Mary—and drove her the fifteen miles to Candelo where she was met by Sister Aloysius O'Leary whom she noticed looked very ill. The next day was Sunday and Mass was at eleven o'clock after which Father Comaskey returned to Bega. Mary considered him to be a very kind priest. On Monday Mary visited the school, had conferences and gave instructions to the sisters even though she was not well. Tuesday saw her again in the school where she gave the children a half holiday so that she could give instructions to the sisters and have conferences with each of them. She did have time, however, to have a photo taken with the sisters and children. Later she went to bed to avoid visitors so that she would have time to finish talking to the sisters. Mary needed a rest because she left the next day for Eden. This was Mary's first visit to Candelo, opened in January the previous year, and she was anxious to spend time in the school to assess the progress of the children.

On Wednesday, 7 August she left at nine o'clock for Eden, driven by Tom Gibbs. They called at Pambula but the parish priest was not at home. After a five-hour journey they arrived at Eden at two o'clock. As she was to return to Pambula the next day she did not visit the Eden school that day, having spent a lengthy visit there in 1899. She did have a conference with each sister and gave instructions. The following morning she examined school books and was ready for the school children when they arrived. She spent two hours there and then prepared to return to Pambula, again being driven by Tom Gibbs. There she saw Father Conway and talked about a proposed site for a convent and school. Did this mean that she was thinking of sending the sisters to set up a school at Pambula?

Mary spent the night at Jim Teir's Club Hotel at Pambula so that she could catch the early morning coach to Bombala.[3] The landlady of the hotel, Mrs Schafer, did not charge her and actually gave her five shillings. Father Conway paid her £1 coach fare to Bombala. It was an eight o'clock start and the coach did not reach Bombala until seven o'clock that evening. They travelled the old road up Big Jack Mountain, a long, steep journey which took eleven hours and Mary arrived very tired and cold. The coach had to make several stops to change horses and one of these places was the *Robbie Burns Hotel* at Wyndham where her visit is still recalled.

Robbie Burns Hotel, Wyndham NSW. 2014. Provided by Bernadette O'Sullivan rsj. Used with permission.

---

3. John Liston, *Schooldays by the Sea: 100 years of education at St. Joseph's, Eden* (Pambula, NSW: Excell Printing, c 1991), 14.

After a night's sleep Mary met with Father Norris, parish priest of Bombala, then interviewed some of the sisters and gave them instructions. Because Father Norris had to go to Cathcart for Sunday Mass, she and the sisters had Rosary in the school with the children after which she continued her interviews with the sisters. No doubt, Mary discussed with Father Norris the erection of a convent at Nimitybelle which was in the Bombala parish. Sister Killian, the only sister named in the diary gave Mary a donation. When Monday dawned she visited the school and gave the children a half holiday. She was very pleased with all she saw especially checking to see if the repairs that she had instigated during her previous visit had been completed. In the afternoon, she examined books and received some visitors.

Leaving Bombala she began the long journey back to Sydney, starting at half past seven by coach for Cooma. There she caught the train to Bungendore where this time Sister Clare met her with Father O'Driscoll's horse and buggy. This was an overnight stop and at seven the next morning she and Sister Ann Joseph caught the seven o'clock train bound for Sydney. They were accompanied by a crate of live turkeys raised by the Bungendore sisters and these were to provide food for the sisters at the Mother House. At Mittagong, Sisters M Josephine and M Columba met the train to see Mary and collect Sister Ann Joseph.

Sisters M. Lucy and Marcella met Mary and the turkeys at Redfern. To get themselves and the turkeys back to North Sydney they took a cab to the Quay, boarded the ferry to Milson's Point and took another cab to North Sydney. This had been another long day for Mary but she had to be ready for the next day, the Feast of the Assumption, when a Reception and Profession Ceremony took place at three o'clock, a very busy day as there were many visitors.

What a woman! She was fifty-nine years of age, not in good health, and this three-week round trip had taken her over some of the roughest roads in the country and the longest coach rides, climbed some of the steepest mountains and all in bitterly cold winter weather. She was never daunted by any of this and her time was devoted to the sisters, the children, their parents, the parish priests and the many visitors who flocked to see her and those whom she took time to visit. All this she did to preserve the unity of her sisters and to see to their wellbeing.

A few days later she was at Villa Maria when she received news that Uncle Peter MacKillop had died in Queensland. Her sister Annie MacKillop had taken the train from Sydney to Queensland to be with him. Annie was very fond of Uncle Peter and he left money to her in his will, but Mary and the Sisters of St Joseph were not so favoured. He did leave money to the Sisters of the Good Shepherd where Lexie MacKillop had been a member. Uncle Peter was always kind to Mary whenever she stayed at his home 'Melrose' but did he still resent the fact that Mary and Father Woods had followed, as he thought, a wild dream in founding a religious congregation different from the enclosed European type where the members lived behind high walls and did not go about the streets begging for food and money?

In September, Mary went again to Melbourne and then to Adelaide. She was certainly fulfilling her aim of visiting every convent and not just once but twice or three times. She gave of herself unstintingly, encouraging her sisters to be the kind of women she wanted them to be, united, loving and charitable.

Chapter Fourteen
Other Foundations in 1901 and 1902

Towards the end of January 1901 the Sisters of St Joseph accepted an invitation to take charge of the catholic school at Canterbury. A convent was purchased by Mary and the sisters in Fore Street Canterbury. The Vincentian Fathers had charge of the parish of Ashfield of which Canterbury was a part.[1] Mary wrote to Sister Laurence O'Brien in March and told her that 'Drummoyne and Canterbury Schools (Convents our own) are doing well'.[2]

St Joseph's Convent Canterbury NSW. c.1906.

---

1. Burford, *Unfurrowed Fields*, 82.
2. Mary MacKillop to Sister Laurence O'Brien, 11 March 1901.

The school was called St. Anthony's and the usual high standard of education was imparted, including, of course, preparations for concerts. One such was reported in *The Catholic Press* in December 1902 and gave a full account of the evening's entertainment in which the seventy pupils of the school took part. Following Mary's instruction regarding dress, the reporter described that of the girls who were

> prettily attired in white dresses with pale blue sashes, carrying wreaths of flowers, and the boys flags... The Rev Father Quinn ... expressed himself delighted with the entertainment, and eulogised the Sisters of St. Joseph for the splendid training they were imparting to the children.[3]

Sister Berchmans Cullen was the first principal at this school and when the pupils learnt that she was leaving in June 1904 (to go to a new opening at Warialda) they expressed their love and esteem 'in a presentation of a handsome fitted, writing desk, with an address'.[4] Sister Berchmans had made a wonderful impression on her pupils, past and present.

Canterbury was the only foundation in New South Wales in 1901 and Nimitybelle would have been another had the convent been ready for the sisters.[5] In between her two visits to Bombala in 1899 and 1901, Mary had written to Father Norris on 22 May 1900 about Cardinal Moran's desire to meet the wishes of the good people of Nimitybelle that the Sisters of St Joseph would take charge of the school there early the next year. She proposed that the convent be built near the church, as she did not wish the sisters to have to walk up the hill to the school which was in the church, a church that was opened in 1865. She suggested that the people should build a six–room house or cottage. She had a community prepared to begin in 1901 but only if the convent was ready.[6] However, it was not until 26 January 1902 that the foundation stone was blessed and laid in place by Rev Father Gunning of Cooma who had been deputed by Cardinal Moran to perform the ceremony. People came from Cooma, Bombala, Delegate and the surrounding districts for the occasion.[7]

---

3. *The Catholic Press*, 24 December 1902, 17.
4. *The Catholic Press*, 23 June 1904, 23.
5. Nimitybelle later spelt as Nimmitabel.
6. Mary MacKillop to Father Norris, 22 May 1900.
7. *Sydney Morning Herald*, 29 January 1902, 8.

Then came the announcement:

> For some weeks past, the committee of the Nimitybelle convent have been very busy making preparations for the opening of the building at Nimitybelle, and which has just been completed... The convent which has a stone foundation, is a weatherboard structure... situated upon a hill just outside the township of Nimitybelle, and is close to the Roman Catholic Church and the Nimitybelle Public School. The house contains five large rooms, which are also very lofty, and each well ventilated. This will tend to make the convent a very cool building during the summer, while it will be warm in the winter. There is no school room for the Nuns to teach the children in the convent, but they will receive their lessons in the Church for a while... The Sisters are of St Joseph's order and there will be three at Nimitybelle. Although the Sisters have arrived and taken over their duties they will not be actively engaged in tuition till Monday next, 12th May.[8]

Mary had passed through Nimitybelle on Tuesday, 19 April 1899, and mentioned in her diary that she had a free dinner there. Although by May 1902 Mary was in New Zealand, arrangements were well in hand and the community chosen. Sister Colman Cawley, the first Superior of the convent, had a splendid singing voice and possessed dramatic and artistic gifts as well as being an excellent teacher.

Children in front of Nimitybelle Convent Nimmitabel NSW (formerly Nimitybelle). 1902. Photo provided by Ian Blyton. Used with permission.

---

8. *Bombala Times and Monaro and Coast Districts General Advertiser,* 9 May 1902, 2.

By the end of 1901, Mary's health was such that doctors ordered her to seek some relief for her crippling rheumatism and suggested the mineral springs of Rotorua as a remedy. She left for New Zealand at the end of January 1902 taking her sister Annie with her as a companion.

So Mary did not see the new convent at Nimitybelle. She suffered a stroke at Rotorua on 11 May but in a letter to Sister La Merci Mahony on 9 May she had spoken of the new foundation at Rockhampton saying: 'I will send you a letter to forward to her (Sister M. Joseph) and to the sisters of the new foundation, to whom, as also the Nimitybelle ones, I send fond love and blessing'.[9]

Mary had a special connection with Nimitybelle as many of her mother's relatives had settled in and around this district and she spent some days with them as she made many journeys backwards and forwards between Sydney, Brisbane, Melbourne and Adelaide. An extant letter to a Mr McDonald, written from Bungendore on 14 April 1899, regretted that she was not able to meet up with him or to see some of the McDonalds as she passed through Nimitybelle. However, she hoped to see them on her next visit.[10]

The sisters arrived in Nimitybelle in May and took up residence in the new convent. The committee decided to hold a celebration Ball to mark the opening. This took place on 2 May 1902 and was a huge success. Patrons came from all parts of the Monaro—Bega, Bombala, Berridale, Dalgety, Cooma, Little Plain, Umeralla, Countaguinea and Jindabyne. They danced the night away and only left at six-thirty the next morning.[11]

1902 was a year of many new foundations: Bingara, The Oaks, Walgett and following the Amalgamation, the convents of Nyngan, Nymagee and Hillston, all of which entailed much work for Mary, her Council and the provincials in whose diocese these foundations were made.[12] When the Diocese of Wilcannia was established in 1887 the Perthville Sisters stationed there came under the authority

---

9. Mary MacKillop to Sister La Merci, 9 May 1902.
10. Mary MacKillop to Mr McDonald, 14 April 1899.
11. *Bombala Times and Monaro and Coast Districts General Advertiser*, 9 May 1902, 2.
12. This 'Amalgamation' refers to the Diocesan Sisters in the Wilcannia Diocese who requested to become part of the Sisters of St Joseph of the Sacred Heart whose Mother House was at North Sydney. They renewed their vows according to the Constitution of these Sisters.

of Bishop Dunne, but by 1891 there were just three centres and the sisters felt their isolation. Their Mother House was at Hillston. They were unaware of the Decree of 1888 and when, by chance, they learnt that they could either remain diocesan or join with the regular congregation they made tentative steps to join with the North Sydney sisters. Accordingly they wrote to Mother Mary and she negotiated with Bishop Dunne, agreeing that she would leave the sisters concerned in the places where they were already stationed.

Mary wrote to the sisters on 23 January 1902:

> Our dear Sisters of Wilcannia are now amalgamated with us. Sister M Joseph [Dwyer] is there as Visitor for me (as I could not go myself, nor spare any of the Council.) She is delighted with the spirit she finds among them, and so am I with what I have seen.[13]

By March 1902 the twenty-one sisters at Nyngan, Nymagee and Hillston had renewed their vows according to the Constitutions of the Regular Congregation. Sister Ursula Dunning was asked to be the acting provincial of the Wilcannia group. Most of the sisters remained in their respective schools for the time being as Mary had promised the bishop.

St Joseph's Convent Nyngan NSW.

---

13. Mary MacKillop to the sisters, 23 January 1902.

Church and Convent Nymagee NSW. c.1906.

St Joseph's Convent Hillston NSW. c.1906.

In 1902 four sisters opened the school at Bingara, a town that grew up in gold rush days. There had been a Catholic school there from 1888 and the sisters replaced lay teachers.[14]

The Catholic Press had an interesting item in its issue of December 1903 which praised the successful entertainment that the sisters had prepared.

---

14. Burford, *Unfurrowed Fields*, 79.

The immense attendance was a whole-souled tribute to the unobtrusive work of the Sisters of St Joseph in the town ... Upwards of 80 pupils took part—from the tiny tot to the almost full-grown maiden and youth.[15]

Once again, concerts or entertainments by the children were publicised in the newspaper of the day, usually with a full description of the items.

Pupils at St Joseph's School Bingara NSW. c.1906.

When Father Sheridan asked for sisters for Camden he also hoped to have sisters for The Oaks and Burragorang but it was not until 1902 that any were available for The Oaks. One of the original community there was Sister Eulalie Connolly. A photo taken in 1902 showed her with a postulant, a lay music teacher and a few children.[16] Where they lived at first is not known but Archbishop Kelly blessed and opened a newly built convent at The Oaks on 24 June 1906. Father Sheridan was responsible for the building.[17]

---

15. *The Catholic Press*, 17 December 1903, 34.
16. Burford, *Unfurrowed Fields*, 83.
17. *Freeman's Journal*, 30 June 1906, 26.

On 11 April 1902 Sister Josephine McMullen mentioned in a letter to Mary then in New Zealand that

> Sr La Merci has gone to The Oaks yesterday. She took Em McMahon, a postulant and Sr Catherine from Surry Hills, who is over for a change and Sr Winifred for there.[18]

Em McMahon was professed in July 1904 as Sister Henrica. [19]

Sister Eulalie, lay music teacher and a postulant with children at The Oaks NSW. 1902. From Kathleen E. Burford rsj. (1991) *Unfurrowed Fields* p.83. Unattributed SOSJ image, original not found.

---

18. Sister Josephine McMullen to Mary MacKillop, 22 April 1902.
19. Sister Henrica McMahon was Provincial of Queensland from 1935 until 1947.

St Joseph's Convent The Oaks NSW. c.1906.

Walgett was another place to which the sisters moved in 1902. The re-drawing of diocesan boundaries was the reason why sisters from diocesan congregations were moving back into their diocese of origin. Such was the case at Walgett which was formerly in the Maitland diocese and when it became part of the Bathurst diocese the Perthville Sisters of St Joseph opened a school in 1896. Once again there was a change in boundaries and Walgett found itself in the Armidale Diocese in 1901. The Perthville Josephites withdrew and the Josephites from North Sydney replaced them.[20] By the end of that year, 1902, the sisters at Walgett had prepared an exhibition of work and a concert for 12 December 1902.[21]

St Joseph's Convent Walgett NSW.

---

20. *Freeman's Journal*, 30 June 1906, 26.
21. *Sydney Morning Herald*, 14 December 1902, 5.

Regarding the Annandale foundation, Sister Mary Joseph Dwyer wrote to Mary then in New Zealand, and was able to tell her that

> Sister Josephine concluded her bargain on Saturday last, and now we are in our own house in Annandale. The cost of the house is £900. The rent we formerly paid our landlord £1/1/- per week, we pay now in to Sister Josephine, and that more than covers the interest. The house is two storeys, much larger than the one we rented formerly and there is a very large kitchen and refectory downstairs below the 2nd storey. The Oratory is upstairs.[22]

St Joseph's Convent Annandale NSW. c.1900s.

Back in New Zealand Mary was slowly recovering from the severe stroke that she had suffered in May. Sisters had hastened to Rotorua to be with her and to nurse her. Eventually she was able to travel to the convent at Remuera in Auckland. Bishop Lenihan was instrumental in arranging for the move from Rotorua to Auckland and then from Auckland to Sydney where she arrived on 15 December 1902 after an absence of almost a year. Mary was grateful for Bishop Lenihan's assistance and organised for a set of robes to be sent to him. These were made by the sisters at St Martha's Industrial Home. Bishop Lenihan was delighted with the gift and in a letter of thanks made the playful comment that 'I think I shall move about the house with them and go to bed in them. They are so beautiful.'[23]

---

22. Sister Mary Joseph Dwyer to Mary MacKillop, 15 April 1902.
23. Bishop Lenihan to Mary MacKillop, 7 April 1903.

Mary had long wished for someone to write the biography of Father Julian Tenison Woods and over a period of time, she undertook this work herself. Many years later, her work was printed by the Archives of the Sisters of St Joseph of the Sacred Heart and the inside cover contained the information that 'after Mary was physically affected by the stroke, Sister Austin O'Meara, later the editor of 'The Garland', typed from her dictation. This was attested by Sister Campion Roche.'[24]

Mary had begun the work by stating that

> it would seem fitting that a wiser head and a more practised hand should undertake to write the life of Father Tenison Woods. Perhaps a noble work on the subject may yet be produced: meantime it is a 'Labour of love' to draw this unpretending sketch, which will have one great advantage—it will be strictly authentic.[25]

Mary hoped to have the work printed and with this in mind she forwarded a copy to Cardinal Moran with an accompanying letter. She wrote with her left hand, and in a short letter to her brother Father Donald, told him 'I ventured to write like this to the Cardinal and begged of him to read the sketch of F.W.'s Life which I sent to him, hoping that he would approve of it and allow it to be printed'.[26]

The Cardinal refused her request and it was another seventy-eight years before the generation of sisters living in 1981 was able to read what Mary had written. But the work remained—for the future to take it up. In it Mary drew on many sources, including letters no longer extant. So whilst she could no longer take those extensive journeys to visit her sisters scattered throughout Australia and New Zealand, she was certainly not idle. Her faithful friend, Sister Austin, ably assisted her in this work of love.

---

24. *Resource Material from the Archives of the Sisters of St Joseph of the Sacred Heart*, Issue No. 6 1981, inside front cover.
25. *Resource Material*, Issue No. 6, 1.
26. Mary MacKillop to her brother Father Donald, 15 June 1903.

Chapter Fifteen
The Final Years 1903–1909

Even though disabled by her stroke, Mary was not idle where the affairs of the congregation were concerned. With the aid of her assistant, Sister La Merci and her councillors, the convents and schools in New South Wales continued to flourish. Mary's prolific letter writing, however, suffered as she struggled to write with her left hand, or to use the typewriter which she had mastered. Often Sister La Merci, or one of the other sisters wrote at her dictation. Her mind was as clear and sharp as ever and her letters at this time continued to give guidance and admonitions to the sisters throughout Australia and New Zealand. Her circular to them on 25 September 1903, began with the sentence

> It is time I should write again to you, and as it is not as easy to do so as of old, you will excuse my sentences being brief.[1]

In this circular, written from the Girls' Orphanage, Gore Hill, she requested that they fill in a form and give information regarding the schools, and submit account books, rolls, diaries for the years 1900–1903. These were for her to examine and so remain in touch with the situation in each place.

Not only did Mary write about the affairs of the sisters and their ministries, she was alert to the changes taking place in the world around her and when women were given the right to vote in federal elections in 1903, she wrote to the sisters telling them

---

1. Mary MacKillop to the Sisters, 25 September 1903.

It is a duty on us all to vote, and for this reason all must have their names on the Electoral rolls where they are placed. See to this at once.[2]

Had she recalled the time that her father, Alexander MacKillop, had made an unsuccessful bid to enter Parliament and wonder whether the women's vote at that time would have made a difference to the result?

With so many schools opened over the previous three years, the only one for 1903 was the school at Burragorang where Father Ryan was the first parish priest. Three sisters opened the school with forty-nine pupils. The *Camden News* reported in December 1904 that

> the convent schools both at The Oaks and Burragorang prior to this Christmas vacation held very successful concerts by the pupils, showing high tuition and careful training of the Sisters.[3]

Once again the work of the sisters was highly praised in the local press.

St Joseph's Burragorang NSW. 1909.

---

2. Mary MacKillop to the Sisters, 16 July 1903.
3. *Camden News*, 22 December 1904, 4.

On the night of the 4 August 1909, just a few days prior to Mary's death, the convent at Burragorang burnt down. The sisters and the two boarders escaped with a few belongings and with the Tabernacle, as the convent was engulfed in flames. Their next door neighours, the Dennis family, gave them shelter that night and the next day Mr Quig put a cottage at their disposal.[4] The sad part was that the sisters did not return there after the Christmas vacation. But all that was in the future.

On 10 May 1903 Cardinal Moran visited the Mother House to bless the latest additions to the convent. He addressed a large gathering of people and this was reported in the *Freeman's Journal*. In his address he mentioned that:

> They all remembered what a different appearance the convent presented a few months ago. He congratulated the architect on reducing such disorderly elements to such perfect order, and making the convent a thing of beauty.[5]

The new additions comprised a three-storey wing on either side of the two terrace houses and contained dormitories, community room, study hall, four reception rooms, sacristy, kitchen and refectory. These additions provided accommodation for the novices and for sisters coming for retreat. Among those present at the opening was Miss Annie MacKillop.

St Joseph's Convent North Sydney NSW.

---

4. *Catholic Press,* 12 August 1909, 18.
5. *Freeman's Journal,* 16 May 1903, 25.

The Kensington convent was being extended during 1903, also to provide more accommodation for the sisters although the work had to cease because sufficient funds were unavailable. Only the kitchen wing was completed during that year.[6] Mary, unaware of this interruption to the building, wrote to the sisters in South Australia in November announcing the delay of their retreat until the following Easter because

> it would never do to go into a damp house—even if the New Building would be so far advanced as to admit of being used . . . at Easter you will have your reward—and I think I can promise to enjoy it with you.[7]

In February 1904 Mary left North Sydney and travelled by train to Melbourne and then in March to Kensington, South Australia, and all this despite her delicate health. When she reached Kensington she saw for herself the part of the building plan that had been completed. She was with the Adelaide sisters for Easter 1904 and was able to join them for their retreat. Sister La Merci kept her informed of developments in New South Wales and she and Mary were in frequent contact by letter and, when necessary, by telegram.

From Kensington Mary wrote a short letter to Sister Josephine McMullen for her feast day, St Joseph's Day. To what other sister could Mary write like this?

> To my faithful Sister Josephine of the Sacred Heart who never gave me sorrow or pain.
> May the Sacred Heart bring you all the graces and blessings I wish you on your Feast today, and regard all your faithful service in Its cause?
> May It give you patience and courage in your sufferings, and may It bless you here and in Eternity for the comfort you have always been to Your loving Mother in JMJ Mary of the Cross.[8]

Mary did not see her faithful Josephine again in this life as she died on 24 April 1904 whilst Mary was in South Australia.

---

6. Foale, *Never See a Need*, 174.
7. Mary MacKillop to the sisters, 11 November 1903.
8. Mary MacKillop to Sister Josephine McMullen, 19 March 1904.

Sister Josephine McMullen with Mary MacKillop. 1871.

Meanwhile the year 1904 saw the opening of three more foundations—Corrimal on the south coast of New South Wales and Manilla and Warialda both in the Armidale Diocese where the Provincial was Sister Casimir Meskill. As Sister Kathleen Burford put it:

> Until 1887 Manilla was part of the Bingara parish, but by 1894 it had a church centre of its own, being served by the priest from Tamworth. In 1902 additions to St Michael's Church were opened by Bishop Torreggiani who invited the Sisters of St Joseph to begin the school there in 1904, with 104 children on the roll. Soon after the arrival of the Sisters a residence was purchased and converted into a convent.[9]

Bishop Torreggiani died on 28 January 1904. On Thursday 17 November 1904, the sisters organised a 'conversazione' to welcome to Manilla his successor, Right Rev P J O'Connor. Two of the school children presented Bishop O'Connor with a silver mounted umbrella, a silver pencil and an address. A short programme of songs and choruses were nicely rendered by the children.[10]

---

9. Burford, *Unfurrowed Fields*, 79.
10. *Manilla Express*, 19 November 1904, 4.

St Joseph's Convent Manilla NSW. c.1906.

The sisters had organised this event in a short time following their arrival earlier that year. On 5 November 1905, when Bishop O'Connor opened the new convent (recently purchased for the sisters on one of the best sites in Manilla) he said that the people

> would find the Sisters of St Joseph self-sacrificing and most practical, and they did everything in their power for the advancement of the education of the children . . . all their work was done for the love of God.[11]

On 10 July 1904 the sisters arrived in Warialda where they taught seventy pupils in the church. Sister Camillus O'Brien was one of the first sisters at Warialda as was Sister Berchmans who had been moved from Canterbury. Just four years later Sister Camillus died there at the early age of 39 years and was buried in the local cemetery on the 23 August 1908.

---

11. *The Catholic Press*, 9 November 1905, 16.

St Patrick's School Warialda NSW. 1905.

A newspaper gave an account of the first concert at Warialda on 14 December 1904:

> The first concert given by the pupils of St Joseph's Convent School, Warialda, took place in the local School of Arts hall on Wednesday night last. The hall was filled to its utmost capacity. An interesting programme of songs, recitations, displays of hoop drill, and club swinging was rendered, while a special feature of the entertainment was the maypole dance prettily given by the convent girls. The appreciative manner in which each item was received by the large audience was a special tribute to the patience and ability of the Sisters of St Joseph.[12]

In the space of a few months the sisters had trained the children for this first concert. They were certainly expert in producing such fine entertainments.

The sisters commenced teaching at Corrimal on 11 April 1904. A rapidly growing area, it was a part of the Bulli parish and the priest, Father JP Dunne, had built a church at Corrimal the previous year and this was where the sisters commenced teaching with an enrolment of seventy four children.[13] A list of sisters appointed to schools for 1905 named the sisters at Corrimal as being: Sisters Ephrem [Gibney], Adela [Woods] and Alfrida [Slattery]. They lived at Bulli convent

---

12. *Inverell Times*, Wednesday 21 December 1904, 4.
13. *The Catholic Press*, 14 April 1904, 19.

until a new convent was blessed and opened by Cardinal Moran on 27 January 1907.[14]

Once again concerts were a feature of the school year. A newspaper account of the first production told of the long and varied programme that was presented to an overflowing audience in the Bellambi Hall. Such was the delight of those present that it was the talk of the town the following week and a repeat performance was demanded.[15]

St Joseph's Convent Corrimal NSW. c.1906.

Although the names of the sisters who taught at these schools were rarely mentioned in the newspapers, one interesting item in a local paper informed readers that 'Sister Horonomery (sic), of St Joseph's Convent, was admitted to Bulli Hospital last week suffering from appendicitis'.[16] The correct spelling of sister's name was Hieronyme. Mary was involved in selecting sisters for these new openings and was interested to hear about their progress. Nothing was too insignificant to escape her notice and interest.

By September 1904 Mary was preparing for the General Chapter to be held in March 1905 and in her first typewritten letter she, now much improved in health, called for prayers for the forthcoming chapter, and set out the prayers to be said. Sister La Merci gave the practical details regarding the election of delegates and other particulars.[17]

---

14. *The Catholic Press*, 31 January 1907, 19.
15. *The Catholic Press*, 14 December 1905, 22.
16. *South Coast Times and Wollongong Argus*, 21 December 1934, 8.
17. Mary MacKillop to the sisters, 27 September 1904.

A letter in November gave further information regarding the Chapter. These two letters sounded like the Mary of old, brisk and businesslike. The spirit of the Congregation was dear to her and she again exhorted her sisters to

> pray that God may direct and that St Joseph's humble spirit may guide the Sisters who represent the Congregation at the Chapter. Pray that a great unity will prevail, that Charity may shine, and a holy unworldly wisdom influence every word and act. Whoever we are and wherever we may be let self be forgotten, and let God's glory, His Will, and the general good alone absorb our thoughts, deliberations and actions.[18]

This was her dearest hope for the Chapter—unity, charity and disinterestedness and a desire for the general good on the part of the sister delegates.

Immediately before the Chapter opened, Mary spoke to the sisters and left them free to elect whom they thought best 'for the good of the Institute'. The sisters thought that this good would best be served by the election of Mary and she once again took up the burden of Mother General.

She was concerned at this time with the extension to the Kensington convent. She travelled to South Australia but was not at all well while there. She wrote from the Refuge at Fullarton in August 1905 telling the sisters

> Don't be alarmed when you hear that I have received the Last Sacraments. I am very much better . . . perhaps we shall soon meet and talk about what has been a passing trial.[19]

Her good friends Mr and Mrs Barr Smith gave the sisters the means to complete the building. She rejoiced that for the future the sisters would have a comfortable place for their retreats.

By November she was back in Sydney and attending to the business of the convents and sisters in New South Wales. By 1903 Captains Flat was almost a ghost town. The population of 2000 had dwindled to under 300. Nevertheless the sisters hoped things would improve but this was not to be. The convent and school closed at the end of

---

18. Mary MacKillop to the sisters, 13 November 1904.
19. Mary MacKillop to the sisters, 7 August 1905.

1905. Concerts were held each year at the conclusion of which many couples enjoyed a social and, as already mentioned, dancing went on until daybreak![20]

Two Sisters who were there in 1905 were Sisters de Pazzi and Gabriel. An article in the *Queanbeyan Leader* reported:

> A Ball was held in Mr J.H. Byrne's Hall on Friday night the 15th inst. being tendered as a benefit for the Sisters of St Joseph's Convent, Captains Flat . . . At the invitation of the Sisters of the convent, a lot of people met at the R.C. Church at the Flat, to listen to a concert given by the pupils of the convent. The concert was a credit to the scholars of the convent school. The Sisters are leaving the Flat, and will be missed by all classes.[21]

The *Queanbeyan Age* published on 27 February 1906 reported

> as an indication of the backward tendency of the Flat and its population a sure sign is to be found in the convent school having to be closed and the Sisters taken away. During their sojourn here the Sisters made themselves very popular as was evidenced by the co-operation of all classes in promoting any benefits on their behalf and which were always a great financial success.[22]

The sojourn of the sisters at Captains Flat was indeed a short one and this was the fate of many schools in mining towns.

In 1906 Mary began a project that had long been dear to her heart and this was a publication that she called the *Garland of St Joseph* which she hoped would be 'the means to keep up the spirit of unity and emulation amongst our schools and children'.[23]

After the first quarter she hoped that it would be issued monthly and she asked the sisters to try to get subscribers, and said that she was depending on their co-operation in promoting this venture. Mary herself offered contributions to the magazine and she encouraged her friends and other sisters to do so too. One sister who wrote stories for the *Garland* was Sister Anastasia Roe under the pen name Una Roe.

---

20. *Catholic Press*, 2 October 1901, 24.
21. *Queanbeyan Leader*, 29 December 1905, 2.
22. *Queanbeyan Age*, 27 February 1906, 2.
23. Mary MacKillop to the sisters, 1 April 1906.

Mary was very pleased with its early success which exceeded her expectations. However, periods of illness were becoming more frequent but in all things she accepted this as the will of her good God. She still loved to visit the schools when she could as Paul Gardiner wrote:

> She was still a familiar figure visiting the schools in the Sydney area. In 1985 an old Mercy Sister at North Sydney, Margaret Mary, was able to cast her memory back eighty years to her school days at Naremburn. When Mother Mary came to visit she could not leave her buggy because of her paralysis, but she talked with the children in a lovely way from her chair, told nice stories and produced sweets from her tin.[24]

New foundations in New South Wales became less frequent than in the early years of Mary's return to the leadership but when the sisters were invited to conduct the catholic school at Fern Hill (later called Dulwich Hill) she accepted. Since the sisters owned a convent at Fore Street, Canterbury, four sisters lived there and travelled by tram to Hurlstone Station and thence to Fern Hill where they began teaching in January 1906. Sister Genevieve was the first sister-in-charge.

Despite being ill during the month of September, Mary was able to send greetings to the sisters in South Australia for their retreat urging them to be grateful to God for all that he had done for them and to 'be humble, and in earnest, and you won't refuse any sacrifice God may require of you'.[25]

Letters from Mary became fewer but in March 1907 she wrote a letter to the sisters for St Joseph's Day. She used part of a previous letter extolling the virtues of our patron, St Joseph. She concluded this letter by telling the sisters that they would hear all the convent news from other sources. It seemed that she saw her role at this time as instructing them in their spiritual duties and reminding them over and over of all that she desired of them as faithful Sisters of St Joseph whilst leaving the 'news' to others.

In 1907 she agreed to a foundation at Rooty Hill which was part of the Penrith parish and was where her old friend Father Barlow was parish priest. That year a converted four-room cottage was remod-

---

24. Gardiner, *Mary MacKillop*, 456.
25. Mary MacKillop to the sisters, 18 September 1906.

elled to serve as a church/school and the sisters lived and travelled to this area from the St Marys convent for many years.

In the early hours of 20 April 1907, fire broke out in the Villa Maria, Hunters Hill convent and the building was reduced to ashes. Sisters and boarders escaped with their lives and very little else. The sisters found refuge at Mount Street before moving into a cottage belonging to Madame Dubois and the school was carried on in the old stone building until, in May 1907, the sisters purchased a beautiful stone building 'Toronto' on Gladesville Road. They named it Mont St Joseph and opened it as a boarding school for girls. The sisters continued to teach in the Villa Maria School but, as the Marist Sisters had come to Woolwich in 1907, they were able to leave that school. Mary approved the purchase of 'Toronto' with the practical details being left to her councillors. The building was purchased from Mr Hugh McArdle for £3000.[26]

St Joseph's Convent Hunters Hill NSW. c.1906.

For some time Mary had been working on a reprint of the *Book of Instructions* which she hoped would be ready to send to the sisters for the Feast of the Sacred Heart in 1907.[27] In the event that it would not

---

26. *Freeman's Journal* 2 May 1907.
27. The *Book of Instructions* was first written by Father Woods in 1870 and Mary had it reprinted in 1906. It was an explanation of the Rule and contained instructions for day to day living.

be ready she wrote a letter and included a reflection which she sent with her fondest love and her hope 'that it will come home to each one as I often feel it does to me'.[28] This was *An Appeal of the Sacred Heart to a Weary, Disappointed Soul* in which the depth of her own feelings were clearly shown.

Mary read an account of the opening of the convent and school at Bundarra in the *Catholic Press* of 30 January 1908. The parish priest was Father Guerrini and he requested two of his parishioners, Messrs Britten and Broughan to journey to Uralla in their buggies and pairs to bring the first community of the Sisters of St Joseph to Bundarra. On Saturday, 18 January, five sisters set forth, three in one buggy and two in the other. At four o'clock they stopped at Winscombe Station, the property of Mr Britten, where they had a rest break. They then travelled the remaining six miles. Crowds of parishioners came out to meet them and conducted them to the new convent, a fine brick building surrounded by a ten foot wide verandah and set in a two acre paddock.[29]

St Joseph's Convent Bundarra NSW. c.1906.

---

28. Mary MacKillop to the sisters, 21 May 1907.
29. *Catholic Press*, 30 January 1908, 26.

In March 1908 Mary sent greetings to the sisters for St Joseph's Feast. In this she expressed her wishes for them to

> please read the second paragraph of the Little Book of Instructions on the Spirit of St Joseph. It will speak for me. At the same time as this is St Joseph's month, I especially recommend to you 'The Garland'—my own little paper which I hope will do a great deal for God's honour and the good of our dear Cause. I also ask you to do all you can to help our Orphanages, especially the Boys' new building at Kincumber. Help Sister La Merci all you can; lighten her duty as much as possible; she has a great deal to do for me, and does it well—God alone knows how well. I am writing this on the typewriter but Sister M. Austin will copy and send it to you from me.[30]

How useful the typewriter had become. One wonders how Sister Austin did the copying. What was used as a copier in 1908?

In 1908 the sisters opened a convent and school at Canbelego, approximately half way between Nyngan and Cobar, in the Wilcannia Diocese. It appeared that Sister Ursula Dunning, the Provincial, was the sister who conducted the business of this opening with consultation with Mary, of course. Mary was delighted to hear that the sisters were to teach in this very distant outreach from the Mother House. According to Sister Kathleen Burford:

> At the request of Bishop John Dunne, Sister Ursula Dunning, the provincial, agreed to have Sisters available for Canbelego in 1908. The bishop personally took a keen interest in the opening of the convent and school . . . opened on 31 August with 70 pupils and by October he wrote again, pleased that the school was going well and that the Sisters were visiting the people.[31]

The Catholic Press of Thursday, 13 August 1908, reported its opening and mentioned that

> His Lordship, the bishop of Wilcannia . . . will formally open and bless the new convent. It is to be given into the charge of the zealous Sisters of St Joseph, whose coming is eagerly awaited by the Catholics of this prosperous mining town.[32]

---

30. Mary MacKillop to the sisters, 9 March 1908.
31. Burford, *Unfurrowed Fields*, 83.
32. *Catholic Press*, 13 August 1908, 19.

A new convent was erected at Lithgow in 1908 on a triangular block of land given to the sisters by their friend Miss Gell. The *Freeman's Journal* reported:

> The assistant Mother General of the Order, Sister La Merci, arrived in Lithgow during the previous week to be present at the blessing and opening of the new convent and had brought with her Sisters Mary Claude [Turner], Therese [Delaney], Clara [Fitzpatrick] and a postulant. The aged Mother General, Mother Mary of the Cross, rarely leaves the North Sydney convent on account of her feeble health, and could not, therefore, be present.[33]

Sister Dominic [O'Shea], the Superior, invited twenty-two gentlemen to dine in the large music room of the new convent. This was the sisters' way of thanking these gentlemen for the assistance they had given when the convent was being erected. Though Mary was not present on this occasion she remembered the many times that she had visited Lithgow in previous years.

By January 1909, Mary was finding it hard to speak but typed a poignant letter to the sisters:

> Before you go away I must say a few words in type as I cannot speak them . . . God bless you all . . . Remember it is my wish to see you all unless when it is quite impossible . . . today I have been much better than usual, and have been all the morning waiting, but very few came. Even in my chair I can give you my blessing, which I do with all my heart, and ask your prayers.[34]

Why was it that the sisters did not come to see her? The foundation sisters for the new opening at Wee Waa would certainly have visited her and obtained her blessing.

Wee Waa, in the Armidale Diocese, was the last foundation made in New South Wales in Mary's lifetime. Sister Casimir Meskill the Provincial arranged for this foundation. *The Catholic Press* of Thursday, 25 February 1909 reported:

---

33. *Freeman's Journal*, 12 November 1908, 10.
34. Mary MacKillop to the sisters, 12 January 1909.

> For a number of years the Catholics of Wee Waa and the district have been endeavouring to get a community of Sisters in their midst. Their wishes have at length been gratified for at the beginning of this month Sister M Lucy [did they mean Sister La Merci?] of the Sisters of St Joseph Mount Street, North Sydney, introduced a community in our little town. It is superfluous to say that they were given a hearty welcome. As they are satisfying a long-felt want, they were received with open arms. The school is being held in the old church. It was opened on Monday last with 50 children. For the time being the Sisters are occupying a rented house . . . it is to be hoped, however, that the church committee will lose no time in erecting a suitable convent.[35]

Sister Eustelle Albert was one of the original community and sixty-two years later she recalled their arrival:

> Most of the people and children had never seen a nun before . . . we were met by a parishioner who took us to our temporary convent, a rented house in a back street facing the lagoon . . . Our school was the little old church . . . no furniture . . . The men got some packing cases and put planks across them for desks and seats.[36]

Those pioneer sisters endured the frequent floods that swept through the town. Another trial was that their parish priest had to cover a vast area and they sometimes did not have Mass for weeks at a time. Roads were sometimes impassable due to heavy rains and when this occurred the sisters gathered the children and parishioners and said prayers and sang hymns. Sister Eustelle was the organist. Two years later on Sunday, 23 April 1911, the Bishop of Armidale arrived in Wee Waa to open a new two-storey convent and school on the corner of Church and Rose Streets. The blessing and opening were attended by Sister Casimir and the sisters from Walgett were also present.

---

35. *Catholic Press*, 25 February 1909, 19.
36. Burford, Unfurrowed *Fields, 80.*

St Joseph's Convent Wee Waa NSW.

Mary's last circular to the sisters, written on 19 March 1909, ended with the petition 'that God may ever bless you and make you more and more His own is the fervent wish of Your fond Mother in J.M.J. Mary of the Cross'.[37]

In March 1909, Mary wrote to her brother, Father Donald MacKillop, reminding him that

> It is now seven years since the hand of God was laid so heavily upon me. I am suffering intensely with my nerves—they seem to be getting worse. I often wonder how long more I shall be left. But God's holy Will be done, and may He grant us the grace to bear our crosses resignedly.[38]

The remainder of her letter, though short, indicated that family and friends were still of as much interest to her as ever. Despite her bodily sufferings, her mind was clear and alert and she was able to write to Sister Monica on 20 May 1909, telling of her sufferings and that, although she was not able to communicate as frequently as she had in the past, she thought very often of her dear old friend and wondered 'if we shall ever meet again this side of our true home'.[39]

---

37. Mary MacKillop to the sisters, 12 January 1909.
38. Mary MacKillop to Donald MacKillop, 14 March 1909.
39. Mary MacKillop to Sister Monica Phillips, 20 May 1909.

She was as aware as ever of all that was going on around her with regard to the sisters and their works. In this letter she enclosed a couple of little leaflets that she had written many years previously. How precious these were to the sisters who received them.

Mary did not have long to wait and on 8 August 1909 she took her last breath. Sister La Merci informed the sisters

> we were all in expectation of the end for some days past. It came calmly and peacefully about half past nine this morning . . . at the hour mentioned she gently passed away, so quietly that we were hardly aware of it, although all were watching.[40]

Quietly this gallant woman passed from this life, leaving behind a legacy of good works and a life of heroic virtue that, as he left after visiting her in her last hours, had Cardinal Moran murmuring that he had assisted at the deathbed of a saint. He could not have foreseen that a century later she would indeed be canonised by the Church and that her tomb, not far from that very room, would be visited by countless pilgrims who would kneel in silent prayer beseeching her to intercede for them in their hour of need. Her legacy lives on.

Many of the places where she opened schools in New South Wales have passed into the hands of competent catholic lay teachers but in distant country places which she saw opened: Bombala, Eden, Mittagong, Dapto, Lithgow, Picton, Quirindi, Walgett, Warialda and Wee Waa, the sisters still minister in a variety of ways to the local people. The Kincumber Orphanage and the old 'Toronto' at Hunters Hill have found different uses, the former as a Spirituality Centre and the latter as an Aged Care facility for the sisters under the auspices now of Catholic Health Care. The future is in God's hands but the spirit of Mary MacKillop lives on in her sisters in New South Wales.

---

40. Sister La Merci to the sisters, 8 August 1909.

Reflection by Bridie O'Connell rsj
Mary's Final Decade: – 1899–1909

A Time to Reap

In spite of the physical diminishment caused by age and illness, in Mary's final decade we see the many seasons of her life and mission coming to fruition. This was a time for reaping those fields which God had planted and ploughed through her. Reaperlike she committed herself tirelessly from dawn to dusk lest any fruits be lost. Her passion for the Cause undimmed, she gathered and sorted the yield, giving thanks for the good seasons and recognising that even in the fallow seasons the mysterious plan of God unfolded, perhaps even despite human inadequacies—her own and those of others. The perpetual hope which enlivened her heart from season to season glowed ever brighter in spite of her physical diminishment. Mary's flourishing young Congregation provided abundant evidence that the Master of the Vineyard had been at work in and through her. God's dream had taken shape in the vital fruit–laden vines which now stretched across Australia and New Zealand.

Mary's harvest time was not simply a season for gazing in wonderment at the spreading vines. We marvel at her sustained toiling in that vineyard; tending the vines newly planted or well established in near and distant parts of NSW and further afield.

Some vignettes of Mary's toil during her last years include:

Her Public Leadership Role

On 6 January 1899 Mary was elected as Mother General and chose a very personal style of leadership. To her brother Donald, she underlined the blessings and challenges:

> Thank God the Sisters are united and happy. Of course there are many painful crosses and much perplexity to settle matters, but God is good and has brought light and help when all was very dark.[1]

She intended to remain closely connected to both the sisters and their mission and to visit each convent herself. This she accomplished over the next three years, by travelling extensively in city and country and interstate to Victoria and South Australia as well as to New Zealand.

It was Sister Rosarii O'Kelly who, in her later years, recalled three significant encounters with Mary. In Hillgrove in 1899 she was an eleven-year-old when Mary visited her class. While there Mary received a telegram telling of the death of a sister. She blessed herself and said as she opened it, 'If it is bad or good news, welcome be the Holy Will of God.' Rosarii next met her in 1902 when Mary was an invalid visiting Gore Hill. During that encounter she encouraged Rosarii to join the sisters even though her father couldn't afford the costs involved. Many years later when Rosarii developed a serious heart condition she recalled that each morning she would seek Mary's power to face her day's work.[2]

Mary reached out to persons in all types of need. For example, at the request of Cardinal Moran, she conducted Confirmation classes for thirty men in the drawing room of an elegant Presbyterian mansion. On a scorching hot day she called at St Vincent's Hospital to see a patient and from there she was told to go home and go to bed as she was threatened with a serious illness.

In spite of her heavy administrative duties and her constant round of visitations, Mary herself cared for the sisters in sickness and in health. Sister Genevieve related that, when Mary discovered that two country sisters had left Mount Street without their tea, she arrived breathless at the train station bearing food and fruit for their dinner.[3]

The cost can be recognised in her very personal letter to her close friend, Sister Monica, which bears testimony to the huge toll taken by the exertion of her constant travelling and her being responsible for weighty business decisions as well as caring for the sisters. She wrote:

---

1. Mary MacKillop to her brother Donald MacKillop, 18 January 1899.
2. Oliver, *Memories of Mary by those who knew her*, 39.
3. Gardiner, *Mary MacKillop*, 456.

> A reaction has set in after all the past exertions of the last few weeks and I seem unable for any mental or bodily exertion. It is a horrible sensation and will, I hope, soon leave me.[4]

Nevertheless, feeling herself pressed for time she determined to work on, continuing to reap and to sow. She noted that as she grew older and the work increased, so too did her cares and responsibilities.

Following her stroke in New Zealand in 1902 and her subsequent return to North Sydney, Mary began another stage in her life's journey.

Her Ministry from her Wheelchair

Pictures from the last phase of her life demonstrate her ongoing ministry. She managed to write a few lines in pencil, with her left hand, to greet the sisters for St Joseph's Day 1903. In this, she wrote words of encouragement and inspiration for their ever-expanding mission. She advised them 'never to take pride in our schools or works, for they are God's . . . we are the weak instruments.'[5]

At another time, she sent words of comfort to a grieving sister and showed concern for yet another who was ill. When women received the right to vote she urged the sisters to vote responsibly in the forthcoming government elections. She invited the sisters across the congregation to organise fundraising for a bazaar at the Orphanage. And, even impeded as she was, she managed to visit the schools in the Sydney area talking to children from her chair in a buggy.

Mary ventured interstate once again to Victoria and South Australia. She became ill in Adelaide and returned to Sydney more incapacitated than before yet always totally given to her mothering role, including the oversight of a new planting—the Free School at North Sydney, a training school for young Josephites.

Mary's Nobility in Suffering

The years 1907–1909 were a time which showed us her deepest, neediest and private self. She committed herself to honestly facing the pain of life without flinching. As Paul Gardiner put it:

---

4. Mary MacKillop to Sister Monica Phillips, 25 October 1901.
5. Mary MacKillop to the sisters, 3 March 1903.

> Her words of encouragement written and spoken were reminders to the Sisters of the high standard of their calling. More powerful still was the example of her own life. Her manner, kindly and patient, recollected and calm, was frequently remarked on as a sign of her union with God. [Mother] Laurence said she frequently spent many hours of the night in prayer.[6]

To Sister Monica Phillips she wrote in May 1909

> As for my own health dear child, my sufferings are increasing gradually. The nerves are giving me a great deal of trouble. I scarcely know any rest from them at all. It is just seven years since the hand of God was laid heavily upon me, and I often wonder how long more I shall be left in this weary world; but a thousand times welcome be His most holy Will.[7]

The Legacy of her Sanctity

After Mary's death on 8 August 1909, many people came to the site of her death seeking relics knowing that this was a special person whom they venerated for her personal holiness. So the legacy of her sanctity lives on as attested by the numbers of supplicants who flock to pray at her tomb in the Mary MacKillop Memorial Chapel and receive the comfort and assurance that she had given so liberally in life now bestowed on them from her place in God's home.

---

6. Paul Gardiner, *Mary MacKillop*, 452.
7. Mary MacKillop to Sister Monica Phillips, 20 May 1909.

Appendix One
Sisters Named in text

ADELA WOODS	Professed 19 March 1904
AGATHA DOHERTY	Professed 15 August 1882
AGNES BARTHOLOMEW	Professed 15 August 1873
AGNES SMITH	Professed 24 May 1869
AIDEN MADDEN	Professed 18 January 1897
ALFRIDA SLATTERY	Professed 2 February 1901
ALOYSIUS FERRICKS	Professed 31 August 1874
ALOYSIUS LENIHAN	Professed 6 May 1871
ALOYSIUS O'LEARY	Professed 25 December 1869
ALPHONSUS BARRETT	Professed 11 December 1905
ALPHONSUS FORDE	Professed 27 September 1879
ALPHONSUS KENNEDY	Professed 20 June 1875
AMBROSE McGEE	Professed 2 July 1886
AMBROSE RYAN	Professed 24 January 1892
AMBROSINE O'DONNELL	Professed 16 July 1877
ANNE FORDE	Professed 28 December 1878
ANDREA HOWLEY	Professed 25 December 1870
ANGELA D'ARCY	Professed 2 February 1879
ANNE DERRICK	Professed 23 January 1899
ANNE JOSEPH WATERS	Professed 16 May 1885
ANNETTE HENSCHKE	Professed 16 July 1875
ANSELM HYLAND	Professed 24 April 1894
ANTHONY MELVILLE	Professed 23 January 1899
AUGUSTINE BRADY	Professed 6 January 1871
BAPTISTA MOLLOY	Professed 9 May 1874
BEATRICE MULVIHILL	Professed 8 January 1889 Left 1897

BEDE GUNN	Professed 6 January 1878
BENEDICT AHERN	Professed 4 June 1874
BENIGNA HAMMERSLEY	Professed 4 July 1887
BERCHMANS CULLEN	Professed 12 July 1890
BERNADETTE GOODWIN	Professed 2 July 1886
BERNARD WALSH	Professed 16 July 1869
BERNARDINE LEDWITH	Professed 15 October 1870
BLANDINA O'DONNELL	Professed 19 March 1885
BONAVENTURE MAHONY	Professed 1 May 1870
BORGIA FAY	Professed 2 February 1876
BRIDGET HEALEY	Professed 16 July 1891
BRIDGET KELLEGHER	Professed 23 April 1876
CALASANCTIUS HOWLEY	Professed 5 April 1871
CAMILLUS O'BRIEN	Professed 2 February 1888
CASIMIR MESKILL	Professed 25 December 1870
CELSUS McGRATH	Professed 16 July 1892
CLARA FITZPATRICK	Professed 2 July 1886
CLARE GEORGE	Professed 16 July 1891
CLARE O'DONNELL	Professed 16 May 1885
CLARE WRIGHT	Professed 15 August 1868
	Left 1871
CLAUDE TURNER	Professed 7 January 1884
CLAVER DOOLEY	Professed February 1877
	Left 1882
COLLETTE CAROLAN	Professed 9 February 1872
COLMAN CAWLEY	Professed 12 July 1890
COLUMBA GARVEY	Professed 24 January 1892
COLUMBA O'LEARY	Professed 23 April 1876
COLUMBANUS CONSIDINE	Professed 23 April 1900
CUTHBERT DUFFY	Professed 7 January 1884
CUTHBERT WILLIAMS	Professed 3 May 1877
CYRIL (CAMILLA) DORAN	Professed 6 January 1883
DE CHANTAL MURPHY	Professed 6 June 1875
DE PAZZI BETTS	Professed 7 April 1880
DE PAZZI KETT	Professed 19 March 1892
DE SALES O'BRIEN	Professed 3 May 1887
	Left 3 May 1892
DENIS MALONE	Professed 3 May 1883
DOMINIC O'SHEA	Professed 4 July 1887

DONATUS KREUTZER	Professed 19 March 1882
DOROTHEA O'NEILL	Professed 2 July 1886
DYMPNA COWAN	Professed 6 January 1882
ELIZABETH GUNN	Professed 6 August 1874
EMILIAN DEMPSEY	Professed 8 December 1879
EPHREM GIBNEY	Professed 21 November 1896
ETHELBURG JOB	Professed 7 May 1888
EUGENIUS RAFTERY	Professed 8 December 1879
EULALIE CONNOLLY	Professed 21 February 1898
EULALIA McDERMOTT	Professed 21 March 1872
EUSTELLE ALBERT	Professed 16 July 1908
EVANGELISTA CARR	Professed 19 March 1885
FELICITAS PELLEY	Postulant
FINBAR FOLEY	Professed 20 August 1885
FRANCIS DE SALES CONNOLLY	Professed 21 February 1898
FRANCIS XAVIER AMSINCK	Professed 19 March 1868
GABRIELLE JORDAN	Professed 7 January 1884
GENEVIEVE BIRD	Professed 19 March 1882
GENEVIEVE FLOOD	Professed 19 March 1891
GERARD ROWAN	Professed 13 October 1895
GERTRUDE BERTHEAU	Professed 7 July 1872
GERTRUDE HAYMAN	Professed 2 February 1869
GERTRUDE LEONARD	Professed 9 January 1907
GERTRUDE O'GORMAN	Professed 14 April 1874
GONZAGA DELANEY	Professed 8 January 1883
GONZAGA KENNEDY	Professed 6 October 1875
GONZAGA LYNCH	Professed 16 July 1871
GREGORY KAIN	Professed 24 April 1894
HILARY TOOHEY	Professed 19 March 1892
HENRICA McMAHON	Professed 2 July 1904
IDUS McNAMARA	Professed 13 October 1895
IGNATIUS GRIFFIN	Professed 23 April 1876
IMELDA GLEESON	Professed 2 February 1886
JEROME CAHILL	Professed 14 September 1887
JOSEPH LONERGAN	Professed 2 July 1869
JOSEPH MARY BUTLER	Professed 15 August 1881
JOSEPH MARY FITZGERALD	Professed 24 May 1869
JOSEPHINE CAROLAN	Professed 9 February 1872
JOSEPHINE McMULLEN	Professed 15 August 1868

JULIA DONNELLY	Professed 2 February 1888
JULIAN GRIFFIN	Professed 16 July 1891
JUSTINE LUPTON	Professed 2 February 1877
KILLIAN ALLEN	Professed 24 April 1894
LA MERCI MAHONY	Professed 3 May 1877
LOUIS MARY DALY	Professed 17 January 1893
LUCY O'NEILL	Professed 31 July 1875
LUIGI MEADE	Professed 6 January 1883
MAGDALEN DALY	Professed 28 April 1901
MAGDALEN MARY THOMPSON	Professed 7 January 1884
MARCELLA DWYER	Professed 23 January 1874
MARCELLINUS MULHERON	Professed 8 September 1898
MARGARET CROWE	Professed 4 June 1874
MARGARET MARY WILLIAMS	Professed 7 September 1889
MARTINA BUNFIELD	Professed 19 March 1872
MARTINA O'NEILL	Professed in Qld 1876 Left from Sydney 1882
MARY ANN CHRISTIE	Postulant who later left.
MARY DE SALES TOBIN	Professed 14 April 1874
MARY FRANCES GOODYER	Professed 2 February 1875
MARY JOSEPH DWYER	Professed 24 May 1869
MARY JOSEPHINE MAHONY	Professed 16 June 1871
MECHTILDE McNAMARA	Professed 16 July 1873
MECHTILDE WOODS	Professed 24 September 1870
MILDRED BOGAN	Professed 8 September 1881
MONICA PHILLIPS	Professed 2 July 1869
PATRICIA CAMPBELL	Professed 28 April 1876
PATRICK BARRY	Professed 2 December 1874
PAULINA HINEY	Professed 17 September 1873
PETRONELLA WHELAN	Professed 8 January 1889
PHILOMENA HYLAND	Professed 11 October 1874
PIERRE O'SHANASSEY	Professed 2 February 1886
RAPHAEL GEROCK	Professed 6 January 1900
RAYMOND ELLIOTT	Professed 19 March 1892
RAYMOND SMYTH	Professed 19 March 1871
REGIS O'HARE	Professed 18 March 1888
ROSARII O'KELLY	Professed 16 July 1909
ROSE FITZPATRICK	Professed 2 June 1892
ROSE LEHANE	Professed 20 June 1875

STANISLAUS MULROONEY	Professed 2 February 1886
STEPHANIE BRADY	Professed 6 January 1877
SYLVESTER HIGGINS	Professed 2 July 1886
TERESA DELANEY	Professed 2 July 1886
TERESA JOSEPH EASTAWAY	Professed 21 November 1894
TERESA MAGINESS	Professed 23 January 1872
URSULA DUNNING	Professed 19 March 1881
VERONICA CHAMPION	Professed 23 March 1873
VIRGILIUS O'SHEA	Professed 2 July 1899
WILFRED CONNELL	Professed 23 April 1900
WINIFRED HOGAN	Professed 19 March 1870
ZITA NOLAN	Professed 20 April 1890

Appendix Two
Map of New South Wales Showing Foundations 1880–1909

Appendix Three
Buildings at Mount Street North Sydney: 1884–1909

Maps by Kathleen Burford rsj, 'Buildings of St Joseph's Convent Mount Street, North Sydney' (Unpublished Pamphlet, 1996)

Map 1: 1875

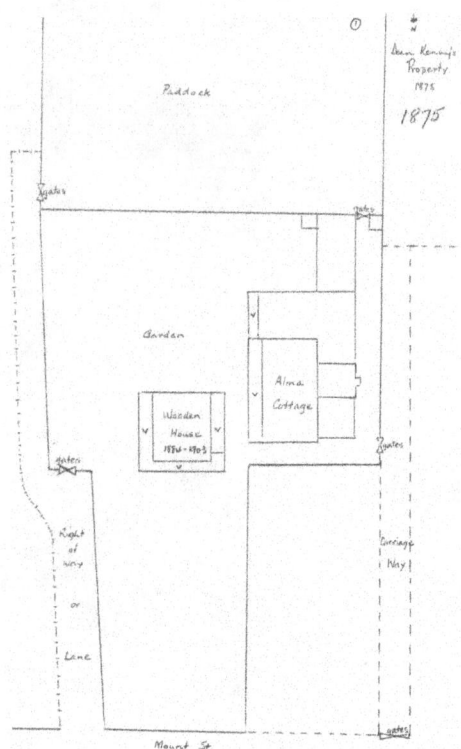

Map 2: 1883

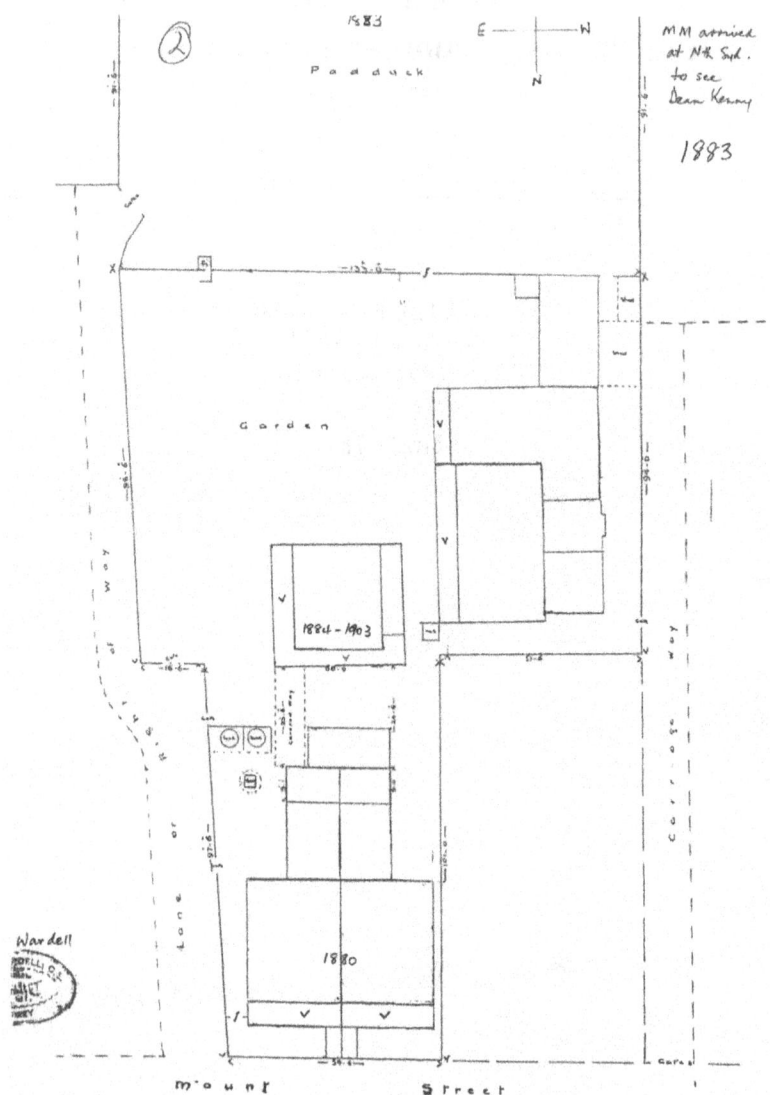

Buildings at Mount Street North Sydney: 1884–1909

Map 3: 1891

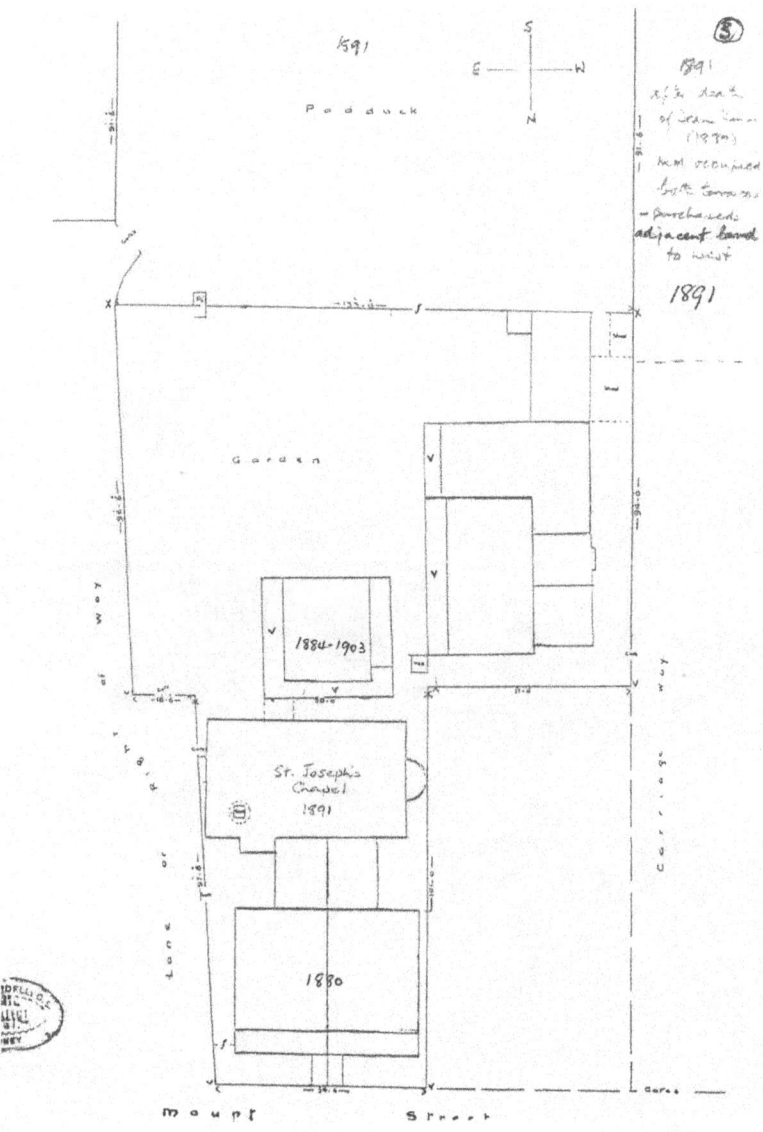

Map 4: 1903

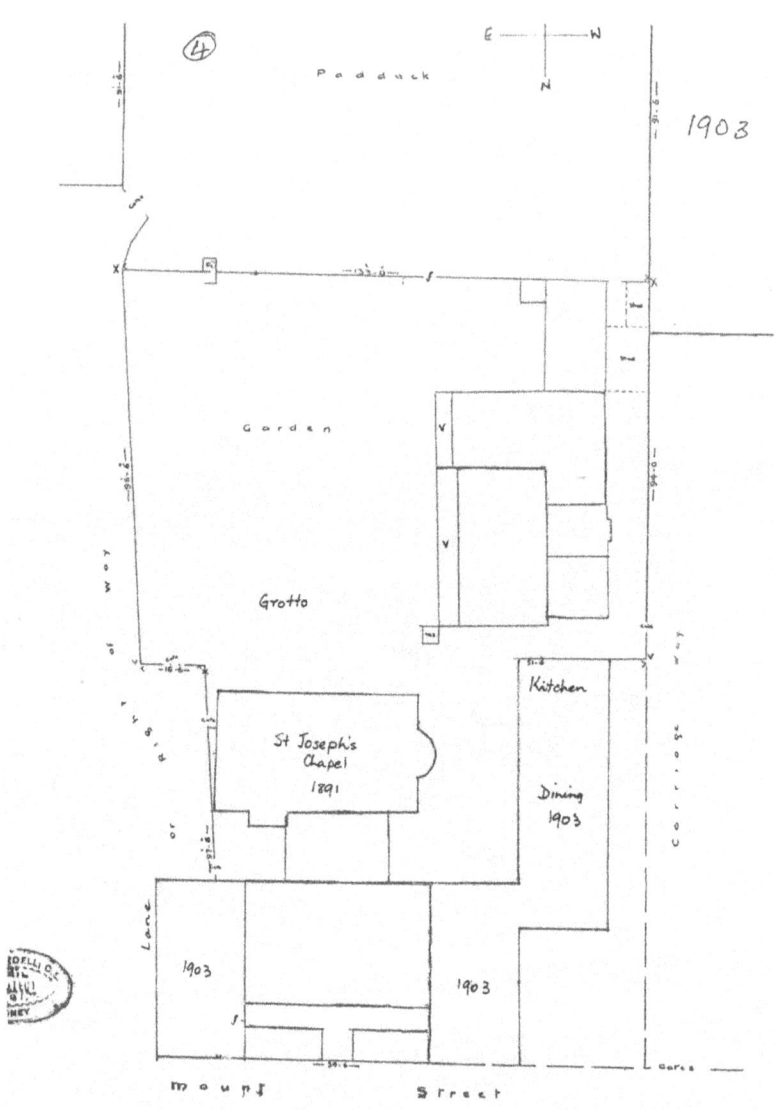

Appendix Four
Means of Transport

Coaches at Penola SA. Undated. Photo courtesy of *State Library of South Australia - Post Office, Penola* [B 15207]

PONY SULKY: A lightweight vehicle having two wheels and a seat for the passengers.

TRAP: A light two-wheeled, or sometimes four-wheeled, horse or pony-drawn carriage, usually accommodating two to four persons in various seating arrangements, such as face-to-face or back-to-back.

BUGGY: A light horse-drawn carriage for one or two people. It had two or four wheels and had a hood.

BUS: This was a large horse drawn, enclosed vehicle. It could accommodate more people than could be accommodated in a sulky or buggy. In wealthy establishments it was sometimes used to transport servants and luggage.

HANSOM CARRIAGE & PAIR: A luxurious carriage drawn by two horses. It gave a very comfortable ride. Mary MacKillop was driven by Mrs Stewart (Adelaide) in her carriage and said it was a novel sensation.

VICTORIA: A carriage owned by Mrs Barr Smith. A luxurious one-horse carriage with front facing bench seats. The body was slung low—front of the back axle. Usually it was driven by a servant. (Mrs Barr Smith sent Mary MacKillop home in hers when the latter was in Adelaide).

Bibliography

Primary Sources

Archives of the Sisters of Saint Joseph of the Sacred Heart, North Sydney:

- Letters from and to Mary MacKillop
- Mary MacKillop's Diaries: 1895, 1896, 1898, 1899, 1901
- Mary MacKillop's Reports of Visitation

Mary MacKillop, ed. *Book of Instructions* (Sisters of St Joseph, North Sydney, 1907)

Resource Material from the Archives of the Sisters of St Joseph of the Sacred Heart, Issues No. 2, August 1983; No. 6, August 1981; No. 9, January 1983

Sisters of St Joseph NSW Province: Our Foundation Story, Issue 4 Photocopied Document.

Newspapers

Advocate, Melbourne, 1868–1954

Australian Town and Country Journal, Sydney, 1870–1907

Bombala Times and Monaro and Coast Districts General Advertiser, 1899–1905

Bowral Free Press and Berrima District Intelligence, 1884–1901

Brisbane Courier, Queensland, 1864–1933

Camden News, 1869–1931

Catholic Press, Sydney, 1895–1942

Freeman's Journal, Sydney, 1880–1942

Goulburn Evening Penny Post, 1881–1940

Inverell Times, 1899–1954

Manilla Express, 1899–1954

Nepean Times, 1882–1962

Newcastle Morning Herald and Miners' Advocate, 1876–1954

Northern Star, 1886–1954

Pambula Voice, 1893–1994

Queanbeyan Age, 1967–1904

Queanbeyan Leader, 1905–1916

South Coast Times and Wollongong Argus, 1900–1954

Southern Star, Brisbane, 1900–1923

Sydney Mail and New South Wales Advertiser, 1860–1938

Sydney Morning Herald, 1842–1954

Telegraph, Brisbane, 1872–1947

Voice of the North, Newcastle, NSW, 1918–1933

Wollongong Argus, 1900–1959

Secondary Sources

Burford, Kathleen, *Unfurrowed Fields: A Josephite Story NSW 1872–1972* (North Sydney: St Joseph's Convent, 1991)

Burford, Kathleen, 'Buildings of St Joseph's Convent Mount Street, North Sydney' (Unpublished Pamphlet, 1996)

Crowley, Marie, *Except in Obedience: the Diocesan Sisters of St Joseph in Victoria* (Sydney: Trustees of the Sisters of St Joseph of the Sacred Heart, 2013)

Crowley, Marie, *Women of the Vale: Perthville Josephites. 1872-1972* (Melbourne, Spectrum Publications, 2002)

Gardiner, Paul, *Mary MacKillop, An Extraordinary Australian* (Sydney: E J Dwyer, 1993)

Foale, Marie Therese, *Never See a Need: The Sisters of St Joseph in South Australia 1866-2010* (North Sydney: Trustees of the Sisters of St Joseph, 2016)

Hosie, John, *Challenge: The Marists in Colonial Australia* (Sydney: Allen & Unwin, 1987)

Liston, John, *Schooldays by the Sea: 100 Years of Education at St. Joseph's, Eden* (Pambula, NSW: Excell Printing, c 1991)

McCreanor, Sheila (ed) *Mary MacKillop on Mission to her Last Breath* (North Sydney: Sisters of St Joseph of the Sacred Heart, 2009)

McKenna, Margaret, *With Grateful Hearts! Mary MacKillop and the Sisters of St Joseph in Queensland 1970-1970* (North Sydney: Sisters of St Joseph, 2009)

McMurrich, Peter, *The Harmonising Influence of Religion: St Patrick's Church Hill, 1840 to the Present* (Sydney: Patrick Books, 2011)

NSW Land & Property Management Authority, *Mary MacKillop (1842-1909) Records of a Saint* (Published by NSW Land & Property Management Authority 2010)

Oliver, Cathy ed. *Memories of Mary by those who knew her, Sisters of St Joseph 1925-1926* (Mulgrave, Victoria: John Garratt Publishing, 2010)

O'Sullivan, Bernadette, *Flora MacKillop: A Truly Blessed Mother* (Strathfield, NSW: St Paul Publications, 2012)

O'Sullivan, Bernadette, *Nothing without God: The Story of a Hundred Years, Dapto 1880-1980* (Kiama, NSW: Weston & Co. Publisher, 1980)

Pryke, Susan, *Boom to Bust and Back Again: Captain's Flat from 1883* (Captain's Flat, NSW: Residents and Ratepayers' Association, 1983)

Joan Ryan, *A Seed is Sown, The History of the Sisters of St Joseph of the Sacred Heart, 1890-1920* (Melbourne: Advent Business Forms, 1992)

Photographs

Unless otherwise stated below, all photographs have been sourced from the Sisters of Saint Joseph of the Sacred Heart Congregational Archives, Mount Street, North Sydney. The item number attributed to each image below identifies the image within the Congregational Archives.

Page ix: Mary MacKillop. Undated. (Item 007C/044)

Page 7: St Joseph's Convent Penrith NSW. Undated. (Item 157/154)

Page 9: St Joseph's Convent Lithgow NSW. Undated. (Item 115/122)

Page 11: Sister Bonaventure Mahony. Image from Kathleen E. Burford rsj. (1991) *Unfurrowed Fields* p.38. Unattributed SOSJ image, original not found.

Page 13: St Joseph's Convent Tenterfield NSW. Undated. (Item 006/122)

Page 14: St Joseph's School West Dapto NSW. C.1898. Used with permission.

Page 15: St Joseph's Convent Picton NSW. Undated. (Item 079/122)

Page 15: Sister Veronica Champion. Undated. (Item 098/046)

Page 17: Sister Casimir Meskill. Undated. (Item 011/046)

Page 17: The Providence, The Rocks NSW. Undated. (Item 415/170)

Page 21: St Joseph's Bulli NSW. Undated. (Item 091/122)

Page 22: St Joseph's School Camperdown NSW. c.1906. (Item 019/122)

Page 23: St Joseph's Albion Park NSW. c.1906. (Item 056/122)

Page 27: St Michael's Church, exterior and interior, 1882. Photos provided by Marist Fathers Provincial Archives. Used with permission.

Page 28: St Joseph's Convent Camden NSW. c.1906. (Item 038A/129)

Page 30:	Sister Josephine Carolan and the group of sisters professed in 1884. (Item 095/046)
Page 31:	St Joseph's Convent Glen Innes NSW. c.1906. (Item 013/122)
Page 32:	Moss Vale NSW. 2009. (Item 401A/170)
Page 36:	Alma Cottage, Mount Street North Sydney NSW. 2016. Photo taken by Sandy Leaitua. Used with permission.
Page 49:	St Joseph's Convent Lidcombe NSW. Undated. (Item 113/122)
Page 49:	St Joseph's Convent Granville NSW. c.1906. (Item 068/154)
Page 50:	Flora MacKillop. Undated. (Item 006/158)
Page 53:	Father Donald MacKillop. Undated. (Item 001/158)
Page 54:	His Eminence Patrick Francis Cardinal Moran. Undated. (Item 027/159)
Page 54:	Mother Bernard Walsh. Undated. (Item 036/046)
Page 55:	Archbishop Christopher Augustine Reynolds. Undated. (Item 003/159)
Page 59:	Araluan church, school and convent Araluen NSW. Undated. Photo provided by Clem Wilson, Araluen. Used with permission.
Page 60:	St Joseph's School Araluen NSW. Undated. (Item 026/122)
Page 61:	St Joseph's Convent Uralla NSW. c.1906. (Item 002/122)
Page 69:	Father Julian Tenison Woods. 1875. (Item 171/155)
Page 70:	St Joseph's Convent Kincumber South NSW. Undated. (Item 008/122)
Page 71:	Convent Bombala, NSW. 1993. (Item 436/239)
Page 72:	Convent Kiama, NSW. 1993. (Item 424-239)
Page 72:	Catholic Church Kiama. NSW. Photo courtesy of Kiama Municipal Council Photographic Collection.

Page 73: St Joseph's Convent Bankstown NSW. c. 1906. (Item 032A/129)

Page 76: School Hall at Bungendore NSW. 2014. Door is from the original hall. Photo provided by Bernadette O'Sullivan rsj. Used with permission.

Page 77: St Joseph's Convent Bungendore NSW. c.1906. (Item 072/154)

Page 78: Official opening of St Martha's Home Leichhardt NSW. 15 December 1889. Taken from collection of images in next photograph. (Item 026/129)

Page 79: St Martha's Home Leichhardt NSW. Images taken at various times and published in 1906. (Item 026/129)

Page 89: St Joseph's Convent Berry NSW. c.1906. (Item 035/122)

Page 90: St Joseph's Convent Tingha NSW. c.1906. (Item 102/122)

Page 92: St Joseph's Convent Eden NSW. c.1906. (Item 040D/129)

Page 93: Students, Sisters, Mittagong NSW. 1912. (Item 033/170)

Page 94: St Joseph's Hillgrove NSW. Undated. (Item 024/122)

Page 95: Marble slab on the front of the Tenison Woods Conference Centre, Mary MacKillop Place North Sydney NSW. 2017. Photo provided by Bernadette O'Sullivan rsj. Used with permission.

Page 105: St Joseph's Convent Quirindi NSW. c.1906. (Item 044A/129)

Page 106: Mary MacKillop. c.1890. (Item 009A/044)

Page 115: St Joseph's Convent Bondi NSW. c.1906. (Item 030A/129)

Page 121: Lochiel NSW. 2014. Once the home of the McCabe family where Mary spent two nights at Eastertime 1899. Photo provided by Bernadette O'Sullivan rsj. Used with permission.

Bibliography

Page 123:	Captains Flat NSW. 2014. Photo taken from the Lookout overlooking the town. Photo provided by Bernadette O'Sullivan rsj. Used with permission.
Page 130:	St Joseph's Convent Candelo NSW. c.1906. (Item 035B/129)
Page 131:	Candelo Catholic School, Candelo NSW. 1901. Mother Mary MacKillop in top row, far right. Photo provided by Jim Alcock. Used with permission.
Page 134:	Opening Day at St Joseph's Convent Dapto NSW. 9 May 1900. Cardinal Moran, in top hat, is seated in the foreground. (Item 085/154)
Page 134:	St Joseph's Convent Dapto NSW. c.1901. Sisters left to right: Wilfrid Connell, Aloysius Lenihan, Columbanus Considine and Marcellinus Mulheron. (Item 104/122)
Page 135:	St Joseph's Convent Helensburgh NSW. c.1906. (Item 035C/129)
Page 136:	St Joseph's Convent Drummoyne NSW. c.1906. (Item 032C/129)
Page 137:	St Joseph's Girls' Home Lane Cove NSW. Undated. (Item 012/122)
Page 144:	Robbie Burns Hotel, Wyndham NSW. 2014. Provided by Bernadette O'Sullivan rsj. Used with permission.
Page 147:	St Joseph's Convent Canterbury NSW. c.1906. (Item 057/122)
Page 149:	Children in front of Nimitybelle Convent Nimmitabel NSW (formerly Nimitybelle). 1902. Photo provided by Ian Blyton. Used with permission.
Page 151:	St Joseph's Convent Nyngan NSW. Undated. (Item 102/154)
Page 152:	Church and Convent Nymagee NSW. c.1906. (Item 102/154)
Page 152:	St Joseph's Convent Hillston NSW. c.1906. (Item 052B/129)

Page 153:   Pupils at St Joseph's School Bingara NSW. c.1906. (Item 077/122)

Page 154:   Sister Eulalie, lay music teacher and a postulant with children at The Oaks NSW. 1902. From Kathleen E. Burford rsj. (1991) *Unfurrowed Fields* p.83. Unattributed SOSJ image, original not found.

Page 155:   St Joseph's Convent The Oaks NSW. c.1906. (Item 037/129)

Page 155:   St Joseph's Convent Walgett NSW. Undated. (Item 045D/129)

Page 156:   St Joseph's Convent Annandale NSW. c.1900s. (Item 038/122)

Page 160:   St Joseph's Burragorang NSW. 1909. (Item 104/170)

Page 161:   St Joseph's Convent North Sydney NSW. Undated. (Item 093/122)

Page 163:   Sister Josephine McMullen with Mary MacKillop. 1871. (Item 004/044)

Page 164:   St Joseph's Convent Manilla NSW. c.1906. (Item 010/122)

Page 165:   St Patrick's School Warialda NSW. 1903. (Item 083/122)

Page 166:   St Joseph's Convent Corrimal NSW. c.1906. (Item 032B/129)

Page 170:   St Joseph's Convent Hunters Hill NSW. c.1906. (Item 043/129)

Page 171:   St Joseph's Convent Bundarra NSW. c.1906. (Item 051A/129)

Page 175:   St Joseph's Convent Wee Waa NSW. Undated. (Item 112/122)

Page 193:   Coaches at Penola SA. Undated. Photo courtesy of *State Library of South Australia* - Post Office, Penola [B 15207]

www.ingramcontent.com/pod-product-compliance
Lightning Source LLC
Chambersburg PA
CBHW070145100426
42743CB00013B/2820